WEST YORKSHIRE
FOLK
TALES

WEST YORKSHIRE
FOLK TALES

JOHN BILLINGSLEY

The
History
Press

First published 2010

The History Press
97 St George's Place,
Cheltenham, Gloucestershire, GL50 3QB
www.thehistorypress.co.uk

British Library Cataloguing in Publication Data.
A catalogue record for this book is available from the British Library.

ISBN 978 0 7524 5292 0

Typesetting and origination by The History Press
Printed by TJ Books Limited, Padstow, Cornwall

CONTENTS

Acknowledgements

My warm thanks go to Stan McCarthy, who has put so much time and effort into producing the illustrations for this collection over the past few months. Stan also helped correct some errors and anachronisms, and made some useful suggestions about how some of the stories might be developed. Though I haven't always taken on his suggestions directly, his input has had more influence on this book than he might think!

The stories here have come from a variety of sources, both oral and textual. Thanks must therefore go to all the people, from all walks of life, who have shared a story with me over my thirty-five years in West Yorkshire. Thanks also go to the library staff of Calderdale, Kirklees, Leeds and Bradford for all their help – the breadth of knowledge and information-gathering know-how possessed by these people is surely an under-rewarded resource.

PREFACE

Welcome to a world of shifting truth. We have stories here that seem completely made up, but just might have a kernel of truth in them; and stories that purport to be truth, but give cause for some doubt. They all testify to our love of a good tale, and preferably not one where everyone except the villain lives happily ever after. That doesn't mean you are on the verge of unremitting gloom and tragedy – just that things do not always happen as might be expected. Anyway, you'll find out as you read on. Please note that these chapters are intended to be read sequentially, as they lead on from one to another, so dipping into these stories randomly isn't recommended.

All of these tales come from somewhere, and although I cannot give all the sources, both oral and written, that have contributed to this collection, I have provided some supplementary information in the Afterword. If you want to know more about the backgrounds and sources of these folk tales from West Yorkshire, you may find what you're looking for there. Of course, if you'd like to pass on some local story, I'd be glad to hear it – please contact me at johnbillingsley@jubilee10.freeserve.co.uk.

John Billingsley
Hebden Bridge,
June 2010

One

ROBIN HOOD AND THE HUNTER

Everybody likes a good story, they say; but I suppose my stories simply weren't good enough for my teachers, who seemed to have some difficulty believing them. Truth is elastic, however, and I was well aware that at some level my stories were true, though it wasn't always the kind of truth adults wanted.

That was always the feeling I got from myths, legends and folk tales, even the fairy tales I learnt that have gone out of political fashion today, like Little Red Riding Hood. They were pretty fantastic at times, and I heard more than a few adults deriding them as 'filling kids' heads with nonsense'. But that seemed to miss the point (as adults often seemed to, back then). However odd, however out of the ordinary they seemed, there still remained the sense that these stories were in some measure expressing the truth, or at least a truth. The kind of truth varied from tale to tale. I later learned that a legend is defined as 'a tale told as if true', and that description, as the idiom goes, rings true itself.

How are we to treat King Arthur in this rationalist age? Or Robin Hood, or fairies, or visitations from the other side of the grave? Not disrespectfully, I would hope, for such stories have been expressions of reality in cultures all over the world for centuries and it is not for us to gainsay their experience. Even if the stories differ from what we read in our history or science books, it does not mean they have no substance or that they are nonsense.

I didn't have a problem with these varieties of truth when I was younger, and I still don't. Yet I recognised that some stories came across as rather deeper in meaning than others, and I came to recognise the influence of the 'great wheel' of myth. Other tales appeared more far-fetched than others, and were not usually located anywhere in particular. Later I realised that these were the so-called fairytales, even though fairies never appeared in them. Others stretched credulity for sure, but not past breaking point – not for me, anyway. These were legends, stories told about places or people, frequently featuring some magical or supernatural happening and generally treated as 'just a story'. But I often wondered – is this really 'just a story'?

When I came to West Yorkshire in 1975, I began hearing all sorts of stories about the valley that had come to be my home, and still is. A boundary stone that twirled about at New Year, a town whose legendary history is built upon a severed human head, an affluent witch who could turn into a deer, or another who preferred cat form, and a man who drops dead as he makes fun of a boggart supposed to haunt the spot. Some of these motifs are familiar and appear in stories all over the world; others are more local and distinctive. But even the familiar motifs raised the questions, 'Where did they come from? Why here?' Poignantly at times, I wondered if the traditional tales had all been made, and survive uncertainly in the modern educational climate of reason and the dramatic, individualistic, climate of performance. In other words, are there any traditional tales in the making, and if so, what would be the stimulus for their genesis?

And then something happened that was rather odd, or it seemed so at the time. It wasn't the first strange experience I'd had, nor will it be the last I'm sure, but it was a singular incident and has lingered with me.

The Day I Met the Wild Hunt

I was walking up Cragg Road – that's the B6138 that leads south out of Mytholmroyd towards the remote moors of Blackstone Edge, on the boundary between Lancashire and West Yorkshire. Just as you leave Mytholmroyd, you pass a sign that declares, 'Start of longest continual gradient in England. Rises 968 feet over 5½ miles', so you know you've got a long climb ahead of you if you go all the way up to the Rochdale Road at the top. I wasn't going that far, though, as I had been invited to dinner at a friend's house in the village of Cragg Vale, a couple of miles up.

Mytholmroyd runs out after a few hundred yards, and from then on there are just scattered houses until you reach Cragg Vale. As you climb, the valley closes in around you, especially on your left, and soon you are walking at the foot of a steep, wooded slope. On your right the valley is a little wider for a while, and Cragg Brook and a few fields separate you from the woods and hills on that side. However, they soon begin to close in and you're walking by the road with the river just below you and the hills just above you; on the whole it's very attractive.

Shortly before you reach the village, the woods on your left part and you can look up towards a rock outcrop at the top of the slope where a couple of great piers of rock, like diving boards, jut out at a giddying height. The largest of these piers acquired the name Long Tom in the early twentieth century, after a type of French 155mm cannon used by the South Africans in the Boer War. The whole outcrop, though, has an older name – Robin Hood Rocks. A pub in the valley below echoes Robin's association with this spot, as its sign bears a customary rhyme: 'Ye archers and ye bowmen good, come in and drink with Robin Hood; if Robin to the fête has gone, then share a cup with Little John'.

You can't live in West Yorkshire long before you come across Robin Hood. Popular association may put him in Nottingham, but traditional tales and ballads lay just as strong, if not stronger, an association with West Yorkshire – or the West Riding as was, to be more exact. Moreover, Robin pops up in place names all over the county and there's a particular focus in the Calder valley, as we'll see later in this book. In popular thought he's an outlaw with certain redeeming characteristics; in legends, his activities are much wider and include tossing great boulders around the countryside – but we'll come back to those later. In whatever guise we find him, he is a figure of the wildwoods and inevitably lives by hunting, often, as the ballads tell, of the 'king's wild deer'.

So on this day – it was a Friday evening early in December 1980 – I was walking along and gazing up at Robin Hood Rocks and I saw that their outline against the sky neatly cut through the constellation of Orion the Hunter, as if Orion himself were sitting on the rocks. I found myself recalling not Robin the Outlaw, not Robin the Stone-Shifter, but Robin the Hunter because it was 6 December – one of the dates known across Western Europe as a night when the 'Wild Hunt' rides.

The Wild Hunt is a spectral pack of hounds that careers through the air, sometimes with an equally spectral giant huntsman, making a ghastly racket. It's also known in West Yorkshire as the Gabriel Ratchets and it's not something you'd care to encounter. No matter the country or culture in which you meet the Wild Hunt, it brings with it doom, illness, death or some unwelcome news. It's usually heard at night, mind, so I reckoned myself safe on that afternoon. Nevertheless, as I walked and gazed up at Robin Hood Rocks, I was musing on the connection – if any – between our local, giant, stone-tossing hunter and the giant spectral hunter of Northern Europe and the significance of the date that I just happened to be walking past these rocks.

My thoughts were interrupted by a Land Rover pulling up behind me and a well-dressed man getting out.

'Excuse me,' he said, in a more upper-class accent than we were used to in that area at that time, 'have you been out walking?'

'Just up from Mytholmroyd.'

'Oh, well, I was wondering, you haven't seen anything of a pack of hunting dogs have you?'

'Hunting dogs?'

'Yes, a small pack. You see, mine got out earlier today and I know they like running out across here...'

Well, a pack of hounds running free would certainly have caught my attention, so I assured him I hadn't, bade him good day and walked on.

'What an odd coincidence,' I thought, 'what with me thinking about Robin the Hunter and the Wild Hunt and all...'

It was then that the stranger reached back into his vehicle, pulled out a hunting horn and blew three long blasts on it, the sound echoing across to the slopes on the other side of the valley. I have to say I felt a shiver down my spine then. But neither hounds nor men clad in green leapt from the woods at the sound and I walked on to my dinner appointment and stayed the night. The next morning I woke up feeling like death warmed up, sick as a dog and as weak and shaky as a new lamb. My friend was fine, so it wasn't the food we'd eaten and all I knew was that I'd better get home as soon as I could. Those two miles or so downhill were some of the longest of my life. It took me over 1½ hours and several fields beside the road received something unwelcome from me. Somewhere along that road I heard a sound from the woods on the western side of the valley – the same horn that the huntsman had blown the previous day. When I finally got home I went straight to bed and there I stayed, hardly eating, for the next five days or so, wondering what I'd stepped in the way of.

I began to wonder whether I had run into some modern version of the Wild Hunt and the huntsman, and been touched by its doom. They say that people always remember where they were when they heard of John Lennon's assassination on 8 December 1980. I remember for sure; I was lying in bed feeling very ill, and it even crossed my mind whether the Wild Hunt had caught up with John.

It was the next Thursday, when I was groggily back up and about, that I felt that chill down my spine again. In the local newspaper was a headline, 'Thieves Cut off Head of Deer'. The previous Saturday morning – the morning after I'd met the careless huntsman, the morning that I'd heard his horn again as I was struggling back home – some children out walking at Thistle Bottom, near Hebden Bridge, had come across a dead stag. It was directly across the hill from Cragg Vale, maybe a couple of miles from where I'd met the huntsman as the crow flies – or perhaps as the Wild Hunt rides. This deer was one that had recently been released into the wild on the hills between Cragg and Todmorden as part of a plan to repopulate the valley. The children who found it went off to tell someone, but by the time people came back there was less for them to carry, as the stag's head, antlers and all, had been taken off.

On the face of it all this could be down to a simple coincidence: a man, interested in legends, and a huntsman trying to recover his hounds meet in Cragg Vale. If I hadn't known about Orion, Robin Hood and his rocks, and about the Wild Hunt then I wouldn't have given it much thought at all except as an interesting anecdote over dinner. And of course one can catch a bug from anywhere, any time, so that's just a coincidence too. It might not have been a coincidence that a deer died when a hunting pack was lost in the area and it's no great surprise that someone local might have fancied an antlered deer's head trophy for their wall. That person and the huntsman might even be reading this now and recalling their own version of that weekend.

However, even if you choose to dismiss it as coincidence it doesn't dismiss the experience and the impact it made on me. A collection of traditional elements combined powerfully that weekend and once you make the connections perhaps you have – as I now think – a scenario for the genesis of a story. The tale comprises a local legendary figure, a mythological hunt, an animal with a magical reputation and other weird and fateful happenings. Such a story has the credentials to be part of the Robin Hood corpus and to become part of the local mythos.

If legends grow from a real experience such as this, why should they not be told as true? This episode taught me a new respect for the stories and beliefs carried down to us from our forebears.

I urge you neither to believe all you hear or read, nor to disbelieve if it doesn't quite fit your view of the world. In this book you'll meet all kinds of things it would be easy to scoff at. Don't forget, though, that your predecessors would far rather that these things hadn't existed or hadn't happened, and that they'd never have occasion to tell the tale. It might be a duller world for us, but for them it would have been a safer and less complicated one. So ask yourself, why were these stories told in the first place? Is the answer so simple?

TWO

ANOTHER HUNT, ANOTHER DEER AND A WITCH

The Wild Hunt that we may have met in the previous chapter wasn't known as that in West Yorkshire. Locally it was known as the Gabriel Ratchets, or Gabble Hounds, the shrieking pack that trails doom across the skies on fateful nights. To some people the huntsman was Odin, to others he was the Devil. To others still, local figures took the role and why not Robin Hood in Cragg Vale? However, the hounds came to be known by the name of Gabriel, regardless of the huntsman's identity, across most of Northern England. Some say the origin of this label was not Gabriel, but an old word meaning 'corpse'. It's hard to feel anything other than apprehension amongst such company.

Oliver Heywood, the renowned Halifax Nonconformist minister, knew of the fearful hounds and remarked that they had been heard several times in the winter of 1664-65. The noise of the Ratchets, he wrote in his diary, 'is as if a great number of whelps were barking and howling, and they are never heard but before a great death or dearth'. Around Leeds it was said to be the crying of children who had died unbaptised.

Nowadays, despite the traditional associations with dogs, some people say that the baying of the spectral hounds is the sound of a flock of geese clamouring across the sky. Whatever it may be, the thing to do when you hear it is to throw yourself face down on the ground till the pack has passed and make sure you don't see them. As they are usually reckoned to come out on stormy nights, this can't make the experience any more pleasant.

The Hunt at Eagle Crag

The Ratchets were, it seems, regrettably familiar in the hills around Todmorden, especially around Eagle Crag in Cliviger on Halloween. There they flew around the outcropping rock – which looks quite like Long Tom of the Robin Hood Rocks – before streaming off south-east across Langfield Common towards Mankinholes. It was said that they then flew into the earth below Stoodley Pike, beneath which the Devil had a lair – but that's another story.

Those ghastly hounds have always had some association with deer, and on Halloween on the Crag you might also encounter a ghostly white doe standing at the tip of the projecting crag, facing an equally ghostly hunter and his dogs. And that's the tale I have to tell now.

The main road twists and turns up the valley from Todmorden towards Burnley, and just before you leave West Yorkshire you come to Portsmouth. Up in the hills to the left of the road stands Bearnshaw Tower. It's no good looking for an old house and tower now though; there was a legend that treasure was buried under the tower and so many people went digging in the foundations to find it that the structure fell down. People still live on the old site where once, we hear, Lady Sybil lived alone, save for the housemaid and the farmworkers. She had never married and was quite well off enough to continue like that for some time at least.

This was just as well, perhaps, as there were some things about Sybil which she might have found hard to share with most of the

men round about. Not least was the fact that had she married, her own property would have had to go under her husband's name and rights of disposal, and that didn't sit well with her. At the same time there were some things most men of her class might have found hard to accept in her, too, and it wasn't just the independence that comes of living perfectly well on your own, thank you. For people spoke quietly among themselves that she was some kind of witch – that her quiet lonely walks on the moor were not as ordinary as they might seem, and that sometimes she had 'funny turns'. Sybil probably heard these stories, but whether she did anything to encourage them or otherwise we don't know; as long as there was no proof, there was no danger. And perhaps the rumours helped to ward off unwelcome attention.

Yet still suitors came and they went, too, disappointed that their efforts were not rewarded with a good slice of property as well as a suitable wife. The most persistent of them all was surely William

Towneley of Hapton Tower. His family had a fancy house, Towneley Hall, on the edge of Burnley, and owned much land in that part of East Lancashire. Not that they were ever remiss in acquiring more – often at the expense of the previous tenants. The Bearnshaw land would certainly have made a useful and nearby addition to their holdings, and would give William something to be going along with. However, we may be doing the old family, and William especially, a disservice. Sybil was comely enough, they said, for any young man to desire even without the lure of property. So William fell, he supposed, in love and the more he was rebuffed, the more he succumbed. Successive appeals to love, neighbourliness, reason, logic and economics all failed, and he began to fret enough to consult a local cunning woman. Perhaps she could do something that might win Lady Sybil's heart, or at least her hand.

Old Mother Helston was getting on in years and was well-versed in the concerns of those who came to visit her. She'd make up medicines for those who were ailing in body, or salves and potions for those ailing in heart or mind; she told fortunes and gave advice, and if she found it necessary she'd even use a little bit of the special knowledge she had. Some people would call her a witch, but she offered her services to people around her and by and large what she offered she worked for the benefit of others, not for malice. It was sometimes hard to tell where the boundaries lay, though. She was respected as a cunning woman by her neighbours – after all, fear or disrespect wouldn't get you very far with someone who knew how to employ spells and magic. So people young and old, rich and poor would come to Mother Helston's door, and William wasn't the first of his family to come knocking.

He enquired after her children, though now long gone, and her health, and whether she was eating well, and he laid a little something on her dresser to tide her over and put a little more bread on the table. She offered him some herb tea and they sat down; after a little general conversation they began to talk of Lady Sybil. The old lady could see what was on William's mind and that he would ask her what countless young men and women had asked her over the years – for a little help in their romantic desires.

But there was, of course, a problem with helping William, for Mother Helston knew well that Sybil was indeed a woman versed in the kind of magic she herself used, and one who much preferred her lonely but comfortable situation to a respectable life as the wife of a gentleman.

'Take my advice,' she cautioned William, 'this woman would not bring you the happiness you imagine. I know her well and I know her ways. I would say to you, leave well alone.'

But he wasn't inclined to take no for an answer, so he changed the subject and asked her how the cold winters were for her and added a little bit to what he'd left on the dresser, to put by in case of need. After a while, the conversation returned to the lady of Bearnshaw.

'Well,' she said finally, 'I'll tell you what to do, and maybe this will cool your ardour a little. It may seem a strange piece of advice, but it's all you're getting from me so take it or leave it. You go out hunting on All Hallows Eve – just you and your dogs, mind – and make your way out across Thieveley. Make sure you have a rope made of white silk with you and that you stay out till the dark comes. Be ready for whatever befalls and do not shirk the hunt. And then we shall see what comes to pass. Maybe you'll get what you desire – though for the life of me I can't see why you persist – and maybe you won't'. And Mother Helston stood up and opened her front door for William to leave.

So a few weeks later William gathered his hounds, mounted his horse and rode out on the afternoon of 31 October towards Thieveley Pike. It was a pleasant afternoon for the time of year and the dogs picked up the odd rabbit, chased a couple of hares, followed a few fruitless fox trails, but raised no other prey. The sun set and they were ambling across Thieveley Moor when a strange dog, white with chestnut-brown ears, ran up and joined the pack. William, surprised enough to see such a strange-coloured dog, was astonished to see that his hounds seemed to accept the new arrival immediately. He decided it was best to ask no questions, especially when there was nobody about to ask.

Very soon the new dog picked up a scent, sounded, and off the pack ran after their new friend. From a thicket and off across the moor sprang a milk-white doe. 'Two curious beasts in one afternoon! I swear I catch the scent of magic around me', thought William. 'Well, the old lady said be ready for whatever befalls, so here we go!' And he rode on with renewed energy.

Now William had a good horse and his hounds were fit, but they could not catch up with the doe. All round the moor, as twilight turned to a bright moonlit night, the creature led them, but however tired they all were, William remembered what he had been told – 'do not shirk the hunt' – and kept his horse and hounds at it.

It must have been midnight when the panting doe suddenly stopped and faced them. She was standing on a slab of rock and as William came closer he saw that beyond the rock there was no land – just a sheer drop into the dark valley below. He recognised it as Eagle Crag. He was close enough that he could see how beautiful this white beast was, how proudly she held her neck, and her eyes glittered with intelligence rather than fear. She was hesitant and trembling on the edge of the crag, but obviously weighing up the options. Should she jump off and trust to providence? Should she run through the pack and trust her speed could evade the hounds? Or was she too tired?

Now the strange dog moved forward and stared into the doe's eyes, and something seemed to pass between them. The deer seemed to calm down, her muscles relaxed, her eyes no longer looking for escape but appraising the situation. The hounds had fallen silent. The moor was still, poised at this midnight hour as if this extraordinary event had dispelled time.

William dismounted from his horse and took out the silken noose. He walked slowly towards the panting deer, and when he was close enough he laid the noose lightly, without resistance, around the doe's neck.

The doe followed William meekly as he led her away from Eagle Crag and along the top of the valley side. Following a very strong intuition he did not head for Hapton, but for Bearnshaw Tower. The strange dog slipped away into the night and soon after Mother Helston opened her front door and revived her fire.

At Lady Sybil's home it was all quiet and if anyone stirred as William led his entourage into the stable they took it no further than that. William tied his horse and the deer into stalls, set the dogs outside the door and waited. In a little while the atmosphere in the stable changed and the white doe seemed to grow hazy, indistinct…

Suddenly, William was looking at Lady Sybil, tied to a stable stall with a silken noose about her neck, staring straight into his eyes with resentful defiance as he made his speech: 'Well, my lady, I am sorry to discover you in this state and I feel bound to remind you of the poor view the law takes of sorcery. Yet you need have no fear of me, for I can assure you of my love and sincerity, and this love will not permit me to tell of this night to anybody. But, my dear, I urge you not to disappoint me further, but to marry me as I have often asked before; and if you will agree to put aside these dangerous ways, then you shall hear no more of it from me.'

She could, as William implied, fare a lot worse than this, she thought, though she would most certainly have words with old Mother Helston later. And so it was that Lady Sybil of Bearnshaw Tower, the area's most sought-after but elusive prize, finally accepted a suitor and married him in Holme Chapel not so long after.

Trouble at t' Mill

The couple came to live at Bearnshaw and William quickly came to understand his wife's nature and love of walking out on the hills. He allowed her a good measure of independence and avoided enquiring too far into her activities. The marriage apparently went well and a child was born, to the great relief of their Cliviger neighbours. A woman who had given some cause for concern seemed to have been brought into the fold of respectability.

Sibyl did, indeed, still enjoy the outdoor life but she was careful to avoid changing into a deer. Deer were much too conspicuous, especially white does. Her preferred guise now was a cat, slipping in and out of people's houses and barns until light began to grow, when she slipped back to her bed. Occasionally she met a late traveller and allowed herself to enjoy being petted for a while. Such nights could be most pleasant. Her days were not unpleasant either, now she was accustomed to her new situation as wife and mother and was better accepted in local society.

Cliviger was a valley of farmers, weavers, millers and delvers. People who live in working farms and mills are not usually hostile to cats, as they are useful to keep the rats and mice down, and they will often put bowls of milk and scraps down as thanks for their work. But just like people, there are some cats you take to less than others.

There was just one such cat that used to come around Cliviger Mill. It was milk-white, larger than most cats and looked well fed. The millers supposed it had a home elsewhere, as it only came at night and seemed to spend more time nosing round than in hunting. But there was something about it they didn't like, and some nights if they ventured outside late they would surprise a large gathering of cats prowling around the buildings, or just sitting in silence, each a certain distance from one another: 'just like those Quaker meetings', the miller's wife would say, 'very queer.'

The milk-white cat was always present when this occurred, usually sitting somewhere prominent amidst them, and bit-by-bit the household began to feel uneasy about these events. They set their lad Giles, who lived in a garret above the barn, to watch out for these feline gatherings with orders to disperse the cats whenever they sat down to their 'meetings', as the wife now habitually called them.

One night Giles looked out and in the lantern-light he saw a group of cats in the barn, silent and respectfully seated as ever. He grabbed his knife and leapt in amongst them, intending to scare them good and proper this time, so maybe they wouldn't interfere with his sleep again. As they scattered, he flailed around with the knife; a screeching yowl told him he had connected with one of the animals. In a matter of seconds, though, the barn was deserted. Bits of fur lay on the floor and among them Giles found a paw, which his swinging knife must have cut off. It was milk-white. It must have been the cat his employers disliked so much – they would be pleased. Now, if it survived, it would surely stay away. He put the paw by his bed to show them in the morning, lay down, and drifted off to sleep.

Come the morning though, the milk-white paw had vanished – in its place was a human hand with a distinctive wedding ring on its finger. He decided not to take his prize to the miller after all, but made his way straight to Bearnshaw Tower. When Lord William came to the door, Giles produced the hand, wrapped in an old kerchief. 'I think, sir, I may have found something of her ladyship's.'

A little while later Giles turned and left, his pockets jingling with what we might today call 'hush money'. The miller never learned exactly what had happened in the mill that night until much later, but was pleased that the cats no longer seemed to meet there and ever after looked on Giles favourably.

In her bedroom at Bearnshaw Tower, Lady Sybil had lost a lot of blood and she was weak and feverish. When her husband came into the room, silently lay the severed hand on the coverlet beside her and left, her heart sank a little. Still, at least she could summon up enough energy for the magic to restore the hand to her wrist. She bore the scar of that night for the rest of her life and never fully recovered from the ordeal. Though things quietened down at home and the couple even had another child – born, as people said long afterwards, with the same strange scar around his wrist as his mother, and as all their future descendants bore – Sybil never recovered her vigour and wasted away.

I suppose someone convinced the church of Sybil's errant ways and though maintaining local respectability ensured certain diplomatic measures, she was not laid to rest in consecrated ground. Instead, she was buried at the foot of Eagle Crag, where William had confronted her and won her hand just a few years before. Mother Helston, who died soon after, was also laid nearby.

So it is that if you walk under Eagle Crag around midnight on Halloween, you might still look up and see the white doe perched on the edge, held at bay by a horseman and an oddly coloured dog; but beware that it is not the Wild Hunt you see instead.

Three

A Familiar Story

Of course, it's not just out in the countryside that you'll find witches and old stories. You're likely to find them both wherever people get together and have a chance to chat. Sometimes that's not always a good thing, because where you get chat, you get gossip. And where you get gossip, you get some back-biting and resentment creeping in. Many's the woman who's been called a witch because of bad neighbourliness and perhaps a different lifestyle rather than a taint of bad magic. Sometimes, as in Cliviger, it didn't take much more than a cat to arouse suspicions in certain minds.

There's a whole area of Halifax now, below the bus station and Woolshops and above Hebble Brook, that seems to be mostly car parks. Some people say you can see the Great Wall of China from the Moon – I know it's not true, but it's just something people say – but if it were, I reckon you could spot a housing clearance project in an urban area, too. Just look for the tarmac. Sadly, we've got plenty of it in West Yorkshire, and plenty in this part of Halifax on top of some of the oldest parts of the town.

There's the magnificent old church down there, and nearby was the Moot Hall where they held the courts that sent thieves to the infamous gibbet in its early days. It's no surprise that people used to say you could sometimes see the headless bodies of the victims gliding through the narrow streets around the Moot Hall. There was also the old holy well and Cripplegate, named after the sick who came to take the waters of the well and seek alms from churchgoers and passers-by. But there was also a terrific jumble of houses, close-packed and unsanitary, which shocked even a government inspector who visited the town in 1850. Back then, he reckoned, if you lived in a reasonable neighbourhood you could expect to live to about fifty-five. The labouring classes of this part of town had an average life expectancy of only twenty-two. Plenty of adults here were much older, of course, but a lot of children didn't make it to adulthood or even double figures.

So this was a poor part of town and from the nineteenth century onwards it was subject to periodic bouts of clearance – some went in the late 1800s, most in the 1930s and then more after the Second World War. If you stand on Beacon Hill today and look down, it's hard to imagine what it would have been like. There were so many chimneys in the town chucking out their smoke and grime that some used to call it the Black Forest.

This jumble of houses was pretty messy then, but it was home to a large number of people. A large proportion of Halifax's poor had houses or lodgings in this area and it was an area that genteel folk didn't much like to think about, let alone visit. It wasn't exactly salubrious but it was a community of sorts, with everything that went with it. People did their chores, scouring their doorsteps, shaking out their mats, hanging out their washing – pity about all those chimneys – and passing the time with the neighbours. Friendships, alliances and feuds were made and maintained. Confidences were uttered, support was given, suspicions were voiced and opinions made known. There was surely always room for a laugh or a fight among these people living almost on top of each other, with their kids, dogs and cats running about all over the place.

Betty the Witch

Cat Fold was just one little patch of houses in this jumble, standing off Berry Lane, next to T' Cat i' th' Window pub. It was cleared away in the 1870s to make way for a railway viaduct. Sure enough it had its cats, and there was a little black one that everyone knew because it loved dropping into folk's houses. It was a quick and slippy thing, suddenly appearing in your house, bright and purring and friendly, mewing and winding around your legs, always ready for a bite of something from the pot cooling by the range and ready to sit by a warm fire or on a comfortable lap. Well, everyone knew her and they called her Tibs because they didn't know her name, and that was because they didn't know where she lived.

Some people like cats and some people don't. Tibs was truly a bright little thing and as she sat in the kitchens and parlours snoozing, she was ever alert, her ears twitching this way and that, picking up on every little sound in the room. Most people gave her a bit of a scratch behind those attentive little ears and a morsel to eat, but truth to tell it wasn't always because they liked her. Something about Tibs and the way she used to look at you sharpish when you mentioned food, or sometimes when you were talking about one of your neighbours, made some people a little suspicious. That's the funny thing about cats; both cat-lovers and cat-haters are ready to accept they're a bit too clever, though the conclusions they reach might be worlds apart.

So some people began to fancy that little Tibs was listening to them. They'd look at the cat where it was sitting and declare, 'I swear that cat understands every word we say'. And Tibs would gaze back at them through half-closed eyes and purr softly. In some houses, then, people tended not to talk very much when Tibs was around, and the scraps and pats they gave her were not so much out of kindness as a feeling of obligation.

They talked plenty when Tibs wasn't around, though, and one of the topics of neighbourhood chatter was the little cat. Some confided that it made them nervous and how they thought she wasn't quite above board, wasn't just the cute and friendly bundle of fur she might seem to be. They gave her food, they said, 'just to be on the safe side, like'. Others told these suspicious folk not to be daft and asked what they were hinting at, but they knew well enough. They knew that the gossips were implying that this little creature was actually a witch, taking the shape of a friendly cat to get a bit of extra food from her neighbours and pick up on the kind of information that people talked about in private. And they all knew which individual they suspected. The gossips might call that cat Tibs to her face, but when she wasn't there they called her Betty, after a local woman who had long lived alone and managed to acquire a reputation as a bit odd. For someone who lived alone she knew a lot about other people's business.

Old Sammy Helliwell didn't like cats very much, or nosey women for that matter, and he didn't like Tibs. He didn't much like how she would suddenly appear, purring and curling her tail around his legs when he started to prepare a meal or when he had a visitor. He was getting on in years, too many of his old friends had passed away and nothing much had gone right for him lately. So he didn't have much to look forward to, all told, and he was ready to believe what some of his neighbours were saying. But he wasn't ready to leave it at that and he wasn't prepared to carry on feeding this animal on the off-chance of keeping a witch sweet. If Tibs was Betty in disguise, then someone had to show her up and persuade her to give up her neighbourhood nosings; and if she wasn't Betty, then it would be better for Betty if that could be shown up, too. So Sammy set to thinking and he worked out a plan to settle the matter.

One night he made some dough, put it on his stove to rise and bake and sat down in front of the fire. Now, this may well have been special witch-finding bread, made with some of Sammy's urine and hair, with an iron nail or two and designed to upset any witch who'd laid a spell on him. Anyway, sure enough, after a while Sammy felt something brush his legs and the little cat jumped up on a stool beside him, gazing at the fire and purring softly. Sammy ignored her and side-by-side they watched the fire as the smell of warm dough filled the room – though perhaps this dough was a little more sour than usual. From time to time Sammy noticed Tibs glance up at him, but he took no notice and he left that loaf rather longer than you should. Beside him, Tibs began to get a bit restless, shifting her position and suddenly sitting up and washing herself all down one side. Her purring

had stopped. Sammy didn't move, but still stared into the fire, and then he thought he heard something. He was sure he heard a small voice, and he was sure it said 'burrrns'. Still he sat on and the dough really began to burn. Tibs' tail began to twitch and to swish, she washed herself again and Sammy was sure he heard that voice, only a bit louder, more demanding, 'burrrns!' And he sat on. A few minutes later, a third time it came, 'burrrns!' This time Tibs was looking straight at him, fire in her eyes, tail swishing angrily to and fro and her little pink mouth open and ready to hiss. Sammy jumped up.

'Then turn it thisen, tha old witch!' he shouted. He picked up the knife he'd set by him just as Tibs hissed and flung out her paw to scratch him. He swung the knife at the little cat and, just like Giles in Cliviger Mill, he connected with something. There was a right clatter round the kitchen and the cat was off. The room was quiet. Sammy looked about and he looked at his knife – there was blood on it, he noted with satisfaction. They said that if you could draw a witch's blood, you were safe from her spells, and he'd certainly come off best in that little encounter. He took the dough from the stove and tossed it in the fire; pity he'd had to waste the flour but it had done its job and he didn't really fancy the flavourings. He noticed his hands were shaking, so he sat down and smoked a pipe to calm his nerves. It was then he noticed something on the floor – it was a tuft of black fur and on the other side was a claw and a soft pink pad from a little paw. Sammy picked it up and set it aside, and went to bed.

The next day, Betty Greenwood's hand was wrapped up in bandages. She said she'd cut off her fingertip while chopping vegetables. Sammy said nowt.

The little black cat was never seen again in the neighbourhood, at least not in Sammy's house. Though his neighbours wondered aloud what had happened to Tibs, and some were truly sorry to lose her company, Sammy went on saying nowt.

Some years later, well beyond the age most people lived in that area, Sammy lay on his deathbed. One day, when his favourite nephew was visiting, he sent the young man to the cupboard. 'Look in that theer ambry, lad, and bring me the jar that's reight at back.' The nephew reached into the cupboard, pulled out a dusty jar and brought it to Sammy's bed. He wiped off a bit of dust, peered through the glass and gasped as he saw a wrinkled fingertip.

And Sammy said, 'Now sit thee down, lad, and I'll tell thee a story...'

Four

BOGGARTS!

I don't know why it is, but whenever I get to seriously thinking about local witches my friend Lucie drops in for a cup of tea. She's rather more local than me and she's long been interested in the same scraps of lore that I find so hard to resist.

'What you doin' then, John?' she says to me, peering at my screen. 'Witches, is it? They're nowt to worry about. A lot o' me best friends are witches. Lovely folk, by and large. Though I suppose there have been the bad 'uns.'

'Well, Lucie, you have to admit there have been a few legal cases in the area where witchcraft was reckoned to have been used to harm or kill people. I can't imagine that kind of situation was always one-sided.'

'Aye, there's usually two sides. Do you remember that woman from Manchester who wanted to buy the old Baptist chapel at Heptonstall Slack to use as a coven temple? She got really riled when the old congregation decided to stop her and threatened to come back as one of those big cats, a panther, didn't she? Remember? Don't think she was as evil as the Christian folk tried to claim though. Just a bit carried away with 'erself, that's always a problem wi' witches. And talking of big cats – cats don't seem to be comin' out too well in these stories o' yours, either.'

'Well, Lucie, it's the age-old association, isn't it? Traditional. Me, I love black cats, and if one crosses my path that's a good day assured.'

'Me, too. What you gotta worry about, I reckon, aren't witches, but them boggarts.'

'That's for sure. I was getting to them. Sometime'. I handed her the mug of tea, saved the work I'd done and switched off the computer, settling down for a pleasant afternoon.

Watch Out, There's a Boggart About...

'Plenty around, you know. Or used t' be. You can tell by all the places called after boggarts. 'Course, some o' them places have changed their names now, as it's not the best of reputations. Now, there's two I know, one down by the canal near Luddenden, the other in Elland, both used to be called Boggard or Boggart House and both of 'em now called Ellen Royd! That's odd, i'n't it? Tell you what's odder – both of 'em had a tale about boggarts sitting on a stone in the garden outside the house, both those stones were called The Boggart Chair, and both because they said that the house boggarts would sit on them. The one in Luddenden had even been worn into the shape of a chair by heavy use! That's what they said till some chap came along and recognised it as the old font from old Luddenden Church, chucked out by Cromwell's lot. One side'd been broken off, which is why it looked like a chair. It's back in the church, up by the altar, so I'd guess the boggarts leave it alone now.'

'House boggarts weren't all bad, though. If they liked you they'd do bits of work around the house for you, like Dobbie in the Harry Potter series.'

'Yep, but just like Dobbie they could go off the rails too, get a little drunk on mischief. Carried away wi' 'emselves, like that woman up Heptonstall. Today you read or hear tales of boggarts, especially the troublesome kind. They're still about, only now we call 'em ghosts or poltergeists or summat special. In the past they didn't need different types o' boggarts. If something boggarty happened, it were a boggart, plain and simple! And something boggarty was something tricksy, whether it were getting some household job done in the night, having your blankets pulled off your bed or funny knocking noises around your house. Boggarts disturbed ordinary routine, that's part of their point!'

'There was another Boggart House in Brighouse, Lucie, at Cromwell Bottom. I read in the paper of a ghost there, well several actually, but one of them was a little man with a ginger beard and I thought, well, maybe they've just seen a boggart! Sounds a good description of one. After all, they're supposed to be a kind of brownie.'

'Aye, you don't see 'em often, that's for sure. They say animals, especially horses, can see 'em better than we can and that's why they'll suddenly rear up for no reason – well, no reason as thee an' me can see, anyway. "Tekkin' t' boggart", it were called. There were a reverend chap walking across from Hebden Bridge to Oxenhope in the middle o' the nineteenth century; he wrote a book about it, called *The Wild Moor* and I bet it was wild back in those days, too. Well, he said there was a stretch as you got on to the moor where horses were well-known to take fright at nothing and that was a boggarty spot, no favourite amongst waggoners, I'll bet. There was, he said, a well-loaded wagon pulled by four horses overturned there when t' beasts took t' boggart – the driver had to walk back to Pecket Well to get help, leaving his mate back at the wagon – I bet he were shakin'!'

I nodded, 'I bet he was; there's no danger more frightening than one you can't see! But even when you see one, you might not recognise it as a boggart. There was one just over the border in Lancashire, that appeared as a scrap of white linen and in Elland there was the Long Wall Mouse, a little white mouse that scampered along by the wall and anyone who saw it, they reckoned, was likely to meet with hard luck. Some doctor saw it back in the late 1800s and said it made his hair stand on end, and I'd have thought he'd seen plenty more likely to frighten him than a white mouse!'

'I know the linen boggart, that's the Holden Rag. Now if you go there you're more likely to see scraps of white plastic bags on the bushes. But that puts me in mind of another tale from round there, of a woman at Worsthorne who saw a boggart sitting behind

a hedge at a ford. He was naked, she said, and the size of a man! Well, "That were no boggart!" I thought. But it goes to show that a boggart warning could cover all sorts of dangers, and a boggart down a dark lane could be the "funny man" mums warn their kids about today.'

'Either way,' I said, 'boggarts generally weren't something you'd look forward to meeting, for sure. There are Boggart Stones all over up on the moors where they're ready to waylay travellers and trip them up. They may be worse at night because you could be led well astray, but I tell people, "If you trip on the moors, don't worry, it's not you being clumsy, it's the boggart!" But more seriously, did you hear about the fellow up Todmorden way, near Lumbutts? This is an old tale from the 1890s and it's about a chap called Sam Fielden walking along and meeting a friend of his, Joseph Woodhead. Joe was a road-mender. There he was with his hammers and ready to break off for a chat any time, I'm sure. Sam would bash up a few stones whenever he met Joe – just for the sake of it I guess – and away with the sledgehammer he'd go. Anyway, this day Sam saw Joe working at this spot and he started off with, "Ey, Joe, I've 'eard there's a boggart been seen round here. You seen owt of it?" "Nay, Sam, can't say I 'ave, but I've 'eard the tale", says Joe. "Y'don't know if it's a red 'un or a white 'un, then?" asks Sam, joking of course. But Joe was cautious. "I'm not sure as I've 'eard anyone say owt about colour, Sam." "Oh well," says Sam, taking Joe's sledgehammer off him, "be sure and let me know if you see him, eh?" Sam laughed as he swung the hammer but it didn't fall where he meant it, because there and then he dropped down dead of a heart attack! He was about fifty apparently, and I dare say he might have been a biggish fellow, but I don't know. Folk said after that he shouldn't have mocked the boggart like that, not on his own territory.'

Five

THE MOST FAMOUS FAIRIES OF ALL

Lucie chuckled a little. 'It's stories like that of Sam and Joe that trigger off belief in boggarts and such, remind people that they can't be too careful. Who's t' say there's not more than a grain o' truth in 'em, eh? That's why a lot of folk don't like to use the word "fairies", in case they take umbrage at being talked about disrespectfully. Instead they call 'em the Good Neighbours or Friendly Folk.'

THE COTTINGLEY FAIRIES

'The girls in Cottingley didn't mind calling them fairies though, did they? You know, I think Bradford's tourism people might think about another slogan for their city: "Bradford, Gateway to Fairyland!" That would surprise people, I'll bet.'

'Aye, that it would, but it would be true enough. They've got the photographs in the media museum there to show for it, too. But what do you think? Is it folk tale or hoax – or some kind o' lesson to us all? Especially the creator of Sherlock Holmes!'

'Well, it's a bit of all of them, really, isn't it? Without a general belief in fairies it wouldn't have made such big news, so there's elements of folk tale there. Then there's the fact that Frances and Elsie seem to have cut their fairies out of a book and put them on card before borrowing their father's camera – that's a hoax, for sure. And then there's the whole tale of how the photos took in Arthur Conan Doyle and other members of what we might call the psychic intelligentsia of the 1920s – that's certainly a caution-ary tale. Now, of course, the fairies put Cottingley on the map, something to talk about, so we're back in folk tale territory. And I'll tell you something else too – no word of a lie – a friend of mine, Marion, lived in Cottingley near the beck where the photos were taken in the early 1990s. There were still some old ladies there who grew up in Cottingley, and when Marion talked to them about the fairies, they said, "Oh yes, there were fairies there. We all saw them". They didn't claim the photos were real though, they knew they were fakes. Well, mostly fakes.'

'Now that's interesting! Here we have a small industrial village a few miles out o' Bradford, with a little stream to one side and the local children are seeing fairies there during the First World War.'

'Or before, and probably later. 1917, the pictures were taken. The girls, Elsie Wright and Frances Griffiths, said it was all because Frances kept getting her clothes wet in the beck and being scolded and slapped for it. The excuse that she'd been playing with the fair-ies didn't help at all.'

'I'll bet it didn't!'

'So Frances wanted to prove to her mother that there really were fairies; at the bottom of their garden, in fact. She and Elsie hatched this plan to take photos of them. Maybe it was more Elsie's idea; she was seven years older than her cousin, seventeen in 1917, and the more down-to-earth of the two, though appar-ently she was good at art and had been drawing fairies for years. Elsie's father had just bought a camera and she pestered him to borrow it. Off the girls went, off to the brook and within an hour they were back again, wanting the photo they'd taken developed in their father's new darkroom in the cellar. That's when the first fairy photograph appeared!'

'Which one were that?'

'The one of Frances with five dancing fairies in front of her, with the waterfall in the background.'

'I know it. Aye, it's odd, the waterfall is blurred, as it should be with the movement of the water, but the dancing fairies are pretty sharp. That made me suspicious when I saw it and I can't really believe 'ow anyone got taken in.'

'Well, there is some movement blur in the fairies, actually. Very little – maybe no more than a bit of wind shaking the card – but that's what made some experts argue that the figures were not cardboard cut-outs. Anyway, a month or so later they took another picture, the one of the gnome dancing by Frances' knee. After that Elsie's father wouldn't let the girls borrow his camera any more. He reckoned something wasn't right, but it wasn't until 1919 that the photos started to get famous when the girls' mothers began going to theosophy meetings in Bradford. Theosophy was really popular, especially after the trauma of the First World War, and was open to ideas of fairies. So the mothers said, "Our girls have taken photographs of fairies", and they weren't quite expecting the furore that followed. Perhaps, if they'd had any inkling of it, they wouldn't have lent the glass negatives to the Theosophical Society and then, as likely as not, we'd never have heard of the Cottingley Fairies.'

'You've only mentioned two photos, though. There are five of them, surely?'

'Yep, that's right. The girls got their own cameras, courtesy of Edward Gardner, who took on the case of the fairies as his big issue. Gardner was a theosophist and one of the country's leading psychic investigators at the time, and this is how the fairies came to the attention of Conan Doyle, who had become deeply interested in the world of spirits generally. The other three photos, the ones that really caused a fuss, were taken with Gardner's cameras in 1920.'

'Elsie's wasn't a little girl by that time was she?'

'No, and Frances had moved with her family to Scarborough, so the girls were sort of "out of the loop" of the 1917 pictures. Their lives had moved on, they probably weren't playing with fairies anymore, and Frances probably wasn't getting told off for getting wet.

Still, with Conan Doyle involved, things had gone a bit far, and as they had never confessed to their hoax, they couldn't bring themselves to do it then either. Their mothers seemed to have accepted that their daughters had seen and photographed fairies, and now here was an international celebrity, the creator of Sherlock Holmes, who believed in it all too.'

'No way these Yorkshire lasses could embarrass their families and such a great man, eh!'

'Exactly. So they had to revisit their fairy experience for the bigwigs. They got together at Cottingley Beck again one sunny afternoon and presto – another couple of photos! The first shows a fairy dancing in front of Frances' face, with Frances looking quite taken aback; and the other is of Elsie – looking pretty striking at about twenty years old – with a rather fashionable lady fairy offering her harebells. I might add that all the fairies were female by the way – only the gnome was male.'

'Just like they've always tended to be in children's books, eh? But there's another photo, a third one taken later, that's always puzzled me because neither o' the girls is in it. It looks quite different from the others, just a patch o' grass with very filmy figures in it, even a touch of transparency to the figures. It's called the "Sun-bath", I think. I get a funny feeling with that one.'

'I do, too. According to Frances herself it is completely different from the others, and that's certainly the way it appears. Towards the end of her life – she died in 1988 – Elsie finally confessed that she'd made little cardboard cut-outs and pinned them to the bushes, and that she'd never believed in fairies. The images came from some Edwardian girls' book, apparently. But Frances – she died a couple of years before her older cousin – begged to differ. For her, fairies were real, and she insisted the last photo was real, too. They were expected to produce more photos, but didn't have anything prepared. Then they saw the fairies "building up", as she said, emerging to form as it were, and they took the photo. That last picture, she said, is the first ever real photo of real fairies. And perhaps the only one.'

'So that's why they look sort o' transparent.'

'The girls used to say the fairies would build up slowly and then fade away after a while. They probably thought the same would happen with the notoriety of their photographs, whether they were real or faked, till Gardner and Conan Doyle got involved. There was another chap came up to Cottingley in 1921, a clairvoyant called Geoffrey Hodson. The girls reckoned they led him on a bit, and didn't think much of him, but he certainly thought the area around the beck was thick with all sorts of nature spirits. He didn't come up with any photographs, though, just descriptions. He wrote a bit about them, and then there was Conan Doyle's book, *The Coming of the Fairies*, in 1922. After that the girls were able to get back to more normal lives for some years. 'Cept that Frances was still visited by fairies from time to time, apparently! Then in the 1970s, folklorists, paranormal researchers and media folk began to get involved, so the fairies came back into their lives for the last decade or so before Frances and Elsie died in the 1980s.'

'An' I suppose they could tell the truth a bit more in their later years, since everyone else who could've been embarrassed was dead. Also, by then they were of an age not t' worry overmuch what the world thought of 'em. I'd heard they confessed, but I didn't think it wasn't the end o' th' matter, and you seem to know a bit more.'

'Only what I've read, Lucie. Elsie got a bit fed up with the publicity in 1920 after Frances had moved away, and tried to distance herself from it all. She ended up saying she'd never believed in fairies. Yet in some interviews she seems to slip up and says she saw them as well. Was she, always the older girl, protecting Frances, or was she just denying her youthful experiences, given the effect her claims were having on the rest of her life? Joe Cooper, who talked a lot with them in those last ten years, and wrote probably the definitive book on the Cottingley Fairies, certainly came away with the impression that Frances at least had had some kind of direct experience of fairies.'

'Have you been there?'

'Oh yes, several times. There's a council estate and a new housing development there, and it's all very suburban in Cottingley today. But the beck is still there, and it may be just imagination, I know, but there does seem to be a bit of an "atmosphere" at times.'

'Oh aye, I know! I've been t' th' Isle o' Man and they've got a lot o' fairy places there, and there's some odd sensations in those glens. Can't say I've seen anything though. Not fairies, not gnomes, nor elves nor hobthrusts; not even boggarts. Probably best that way. They're all said to be tricksy. Anyway, d' you know how they used t' keep boggarts and suchlike away from their homes here in Yorkshire?'

'I know several ways, but I know you've got one on your mind so you'd better say what it is.'

THE USES OF CATS

'Cats! Not your fluffy, purring kind, though, least not any more. These ones are rather grey and leathery and they don't usually make much noise.'

'I've got you. You're talking about mummified cats, aren't you? Down in the south they talk about northerners being barbaric, you know. Shutting a cat into a building's wall or roof to starve to death in the belief that it will chase away bad luck and evil spirits doesn't exactly counter their argument!'

'They do it in the south too, y' know! I was on holiday in Dorset a few years back and I saw two of 'em in a museum in Portland! And I went drinking in a pub in King's Lynn called the Red Cat and there it was, up on the wall in a glass case! Poor thing, just a strip of red leather she were, but the landlord told me if they tried to chuck her out, all hell would be let loose.'

'It's been known.'

'Aye. Well, anyway, this unpleasant little custom is known all over and there are a few mummy cats found round here. There was one found at the Mitre Hotel in Halifax in the 1880s, and I

remember when I was a kid there was another one from an old hall in Brighouse – Slead Hall it was.'

'Yes, I've been told of one in the north wall of a farm in Mytholmroyd. Do you know about the one in old Heptonstall Church? That turned up after the great storm of 1847, the one that tore the roof off, and it seems it had been walled up in the north wall there too. Do you know the carving of Old Sal at the bottom of the arch at the east end?'

'You mean the one with her tongue poking out and lots of stuff coming out of her mouth? And doesn't she have cat ears? A friend of mine thinks it's like a Green Man.'

'Yes, that's the one. More of a Green Cat, really. She must have looked a bit scary once upon a time, because I've read a recollection

somewhere that kids misbehaving in a church service were hauled out of the pew and made to stand in front of the pillar, facing Old Sal. Who knows what stories they might have been told about this grotesque figure! Anyway, it's an interesting coincidence that the mummified cat was found in a north wall, the same as the Green Cat.'

'And in a church, too, tut-tut! Bet they thought they'd got rid of such ideas centuries ago. What happened to it, d' you know?'

'It was sold to the landlady of the Cross for 7s 6d. She put it in a glass case, but it disappeared sometime in the 1950s, I understand. I think the others have been lost or disappeared as well. Some people think those cats got shut up in the walls by accident – you know, cats get into all sorts of scrapes and sometimes they don't manage to get out of them.'

'Maybe sometimes. There was a cat sold on ebay earlier this year that'd been found between floorboards at a warehouse in Bradford – Dale Chambers as I recall – and I think that may have been accidental, as it wasn't in a traditional threshold location like a wall or roof. But there's one in Suffolk that was found up in the roof space with its front and back paws tied together, so that was no accident. It's the position that tells you whether it's deliberate.'

'That's right, and it's the same with all kinds of protective objects. You get horseshoes over doors, or stones with natural holes in – hag stones, they call them in some parts, or dobbie stones in others. You also get shoes up chimneys and at doorways, sprigs of rowan in the rafters and all kinds of symbols on the old farmhouses here in Yorkshire – like the roundels that keep off the evil eye, and those carved heads that I'm always on about. The heads were made to sit at the threshold – whether window, door, chimney or roof edge – to keep bad luck or ill-wishing away from the inhabitants, and they're a darn sight more ethical than walling up some poor cat.'

'Ah, but you know well enough that they come from a tradition that includes head-hunting. However lucky a skull might be, the means of coming by a severed head might not be so ethical, as y' put it.'

'OK, Lucie, good point. One thing we certainly learn from folk-lore is that ethical standards aren't what they once were!'

'Thank goodness for that, I say! I don't want someone trying t' stick a knife into me, or my cat, because of something I've brewed up! And talking o' brews, thanks for that but I must be off… I'll pop in again soon, though, as I'm sure I'll remember summat else as soon as I'm on t' bus…'

Six

THE HEADS
OF HALIFAX

THE HOLY FACE

Well, I got to thinking about Halifax again, and heads too, after Lucie left. Many a town has an idiosyncrasy, something that gives it a character of its own, and for Halifax it's the severed head. Look at its coat of arms, which you can see in coloured glory on the gates of the old Piece Hall. There's the blue and yellow check shield of the Norman Warenne family – that's the Warrens, in today's English – and on top of it there's the Paschal Lamb. Right in the centre there's a severed head. It looks like it's being dished up on a plate bearing the Warenne colours. The myth of this particular head does involve something similar, for this is the head of St John the Baptist, beheaded by King Herod at the wish of Salome and Herodias, and brought to Salome on a platter.

But this isn't the way it came to Halifax. The story goes that a group of Christian monks came to this place bearing a great treasure – the face, or head, of John the Baptist. If this is true, in a religious culture where relics – or rather fragments – of the great saints were of immense spiritual value, then part of the body of a

founding figure would have been a huge boon to the community that possessed it. Such relics, on top of the spiritual power they were believed to hold, possessed great value in terms of economy and status. The Venetians knew that well enough for two of their merchants, or rather pirates in those days, stole the remains of St Mark from Alexandria in the ninth century. They knew St Mark would enhance Venice's prestige and attract pilgrims – a good source of regular cash. Even priests were not averse to a bit of skulduggery when it came to looking after their own interests.

John the Baptist's body ended up scattered all over Europe, it seems. No official Roman Catholic source mentions Halifax in remotest England as having a bit; but then no firm claim to his head has ever been established, so who knows! A lot of people have said that the Knights Templar acquired John's head and transferred it to secret locations around Europe. There are Knights Templar sites across West Yorkshire, like Temple Newsam near Leeds, and there are Templar crosses on buildings in Coley and Illingworth on the outskirts of Halifax. You could go in for a lot of romantic and fanciful speculation about Templar influence here, but if you're a historian there's not much to go on. Nevertheless, the story of the head of John the Baptist was popular, and bequeathed a great deal to Halifax. Apart from the head on the coat of arms, the parish church is dedicated to him, and this ancient relic is also said to be the origin of the town's name – a conjunction of Old English *halig*, meaning holy, and *fax*, meaning face.

THE HOLY HAIR

Perhaps pilgrims did once make their way to Halifax and the holy well near its ancient church, and spend their money in the town, because the legends don't end there. There has been a lot of discussion about the town's name, and another popular legend attributes it to *halig*, meaning holy, and another meaning of *fax* in the sense of hair – as in the old Yorkshire family of Fairfax, known for their blonde hair. Only the hair in this story was not fair, it was black, and belonged to a young girl whose fate was linked with that of another religious settler, a hermit who took up his abode in the wild countryside that long preceded the industrial town.

The nook he chose in a clearing among the stony hills offered a sublime wilderness for a devout holy man seeking a place for his own resurrection; a place to erect a hermitage and a small chapel. There he could spend his days in meditation and prayer, and perhaps offer some spiritual solace to any local family scraping a living from the land round about who might be ready for his message.

We could make a long and romantic story of how he built his retreat in these hills, gathered and grew his food and built up a reputation among the local farmers as a pious man who had things to say outside their normal run of conversation, and therefore worth giving an ear to. However, ours is not a religious fable and that is not how the story has come to us. Of this hermit's years in the wilderness, we know nothing.

So we must skip these early years and catch up with him again at a time when people had taken him into their community and would visit him. Sometimes they bore offerings of milk, fowl or other necessities, perhaps in exchange for advice or a prayer and sometimes just out of goodwill. One of the little farms nearby would often send something over and frequently their daughter was the courier.

The hermit had watched the child grow up and over the years she had often dropped in to distract him from his prayers with her childish prattle. Indeed, sometimes her naïve questions unknowingly raised deeper questions for him to meditate on. Something of a rapport had grown up between them. Now she was a young woman, and a very pretty one too. That fact was not lost on the hermit and he debated with himself whether it was appropriate for a man such as he, who had renounced intimacy with women, to receive such a visitor. But he had known her for a long time; he could not suddenly tell her not to come any more just because of something his teachers had told him years ago. And nor did he want to, for as she filled out and became every inch an adult, he became fascinated with the changes that God could bring in every living thing. What a mystery this girl became, and soon he found himself distracted from his prayers even when she was not there. He found himself looking forward to her visits and praying especially hard for the sake of the girl and her family.

At times the hermit wondered if this was perhaps the love that people spoke of. Certainly, when he thought of her he felt as happy as the people who spoke of love seemed to be. But he also knew from his Bible and his teachers that love can be confused with lust, which was a sin sent by Satan to tempt people from the true path of God, and women were created to be a snare for good men. His feelings for the girl seemed to him sincere enough in his heart, but the reactions of his body left him in some doubt. Was this true love? Should he abandon his way of life and enter into holy matrimony with this woman? Or was it lust? Was she a temptation sent by the Dark One to be repulsed by one truly devoted to God?

Perhaps at such times we would think it best not to be alone with your thoughts, but that's hard for a hermit. Anyway, it's just

the kind of temptation that a seeker must crave. This emotional debate occupied the hermit for weeks, even months, and in his solitude he deeply inquired into his own feelings. At last he concluded that his years of prayer and devotion surely stood as some testimonial to his purity of intent, and he resolved to tell the girl of his love.

A few more weeks went by with several visits from the girl, but he found it hard, not being used to it, to speak his heart. The repressed feelings built up in him more and more. He had always been a strong and courageous man, he thought, but here, where he stood on the brink of a decision that might sever his link with his God, his courage failed him.

As he saw her walking down the path one day carrying a basket of something or other, his spirits revived as usual and he thought, 'now or never'. But somehow their conversation, though warm and friendly, never came round to the subject he really wanted to talk about. After a while she turned to leave. In anguish, berating himself for being such a coward, the hermit sprang to action. In that sudden resolve he dropped to his knees, reddening furiously, and blurted out his love for her, his dreams of spending their life together on a farm and raising a family.

Unsurprisingly for us perhaps, the outcome was not as he had hoped. Horrified, the young girl pushed him away and started to run off. But the hermit caught her, embraced her, begged her and kissed her again and again… until he saw her tears. Suddenly the hermit came to his senses. He realised what he had done, how he had betrayed his religious vows, betrayed his God, fallen for the wiles of the Evil One. This attractive young woman was just as his teachers said – the Devil's snare. He flung her away from him in horror; the girl flew like a rag doll into the trunk of a nearby yew tree and lay still at its foot. And as she lay there, so still, with her long black hair around her face, her slim, white neck bright against the dark bark of the yew tree, she looked so beautiful and tempting that again his mind raged at the Devil's wiles. His wood axe lay nearby. He snatched it up and swung it at the part of the girl's body that now so enraged him.

With just one powerful stroke that beautiful head, with the enticing hair and neck, was severed from her body. The hermit, now surely out of his mind, held the head up in front of him for a few seconds and then thrust it into the place where the branches of the yew tree separated. On this strange forked altar her stained head stared out at the world with open but sightless eyes. And the hermit? Staring into those eyes he berated her and the Devil until he was in tears. He strode out of his clearing, out of the wood and into the wilderness. Some days later his body was found at the foot of a nearby cliff. That was the end of his story – but not of hers.

In due course the alarm was raised and people came searching for the girl. Her father was at the head of the crowd as their steps led them to the clearing where the hermitage stood. We can imagine the reaction when the body was seen in the deserted clearing, when their eyes were raised to the fork in the trunk where the young girl's head was staring out so blindly. Her father reached up and took her head in his hands. He tried to remove it from its resting place, but it would not come. The yew tree had taken her long black hair into its trunk, and would not relinquish its sorrowful relic.

So the girl's body was buried, but her head was left in the tree and her hair somehow continued to grow into its fabric. For many years people would come to view this miraculous fusion; some of these pilgrims would take away a fragment of the tree and even bones from the poor girl's skull as the flesh rotted away. Being a yew, the tree lived long, and even the seventeenth-century historian Ralph Thoresby mentioned being taken to see it on a visit to Halifax. But alas the location, rumoured to be at the end of the churchyard, is now lost. Yet yew trees everywhere still remember the tragedy of the Virgin of Halifax, for if you peel back the bark of any yew, you will find slender black filaments like hair – the memory of that young maid.

And so Halifax acquired another legend of a severed head, another origin tale that paints it as a place of sanctity and pilgrimage. Few people today, I'm sure, would lend any belief to the idea

that Halifax was once such a holy place, but the old legends, they tell us different. Who knows – beneath the car parks and the mills, where an old holy well lies almost forgotten in the shadow of the imposing church with its soot-blackened stone walls, where once a yew tree may have spread its ancient roots, in these green fields at the foot of the Pennine hills, who knows what spiritual truth may be buried?

THE HELLISH GIBBET

Or on the other hand, what kind of dark shadow? For growing up with its legendary severed heads and maturing into a centre of the textile trade, Halifax possessed a very particular mode of execution for those found guilty of capital crimes – a punishment that was even handed down for the theft of 13½d worth of cloth. It brought a dark reputation indeed, for thieves met their end by public guillotine rather than by a rope on a scaffold. The gibbet, it is often said, was the catalyst for the famous Yorkshire epithet, 'From Hell, Hull and Halifax, Good Lord, deliver us', which, it must be said, the local people have somewhat delighted in. You can still see the gibbet today, or at least a replica of it. The original mound at the bottom of Gibbet Street was discovered accidentally in the 1830s, along with a couple of skulls, and the model was put up in 1974. From the late 1200s until 1650, the fall of the axe accounted for fifty-three recorded victims, but for the first 250 years they seemingly didn't bother to record or even count the times they used it.

The gibbet was certainly an unusual sort of punishment and it's said that they would have stuck with the rope if they had found a hangman on a day when three thieves had been sentenced to death. But no one had taken the official office and they offered the post more widely, on a casual basis as it were. The town offered a sum of money to a pauper, a tidy sum for sure, if he would just place the noose and operate the scaffold to despatch these three men. But the pauper turned to them, to those who would not do

it themselves, and declared, 'When I have the skill to make a man, then I will hang a man – should it chance that my workmanship does not suit me'. Nor would the victim of their theft take the role, not even, he said, if his losses had been ten times greater. So they tried to set a thief to hang a thief, promising each his freedom if he would drop his accomplices; but each stood true to the honour among thieves and declined. Eventually all three walked free.

Well, along came a passing friar and heard of this situation. He stepped forward. 'Sirs,' he said, 'I have an idea which might serve you well in your dilemma and for a consideration will devise you a machine that will dispense justice without troubling the conscience of a single man or woman.'

This was just what was wanted. 'Hmmm, tell us more...' said the good burghers and the canny priest told them just enough to secure his commission. Permission was soon sought and obtained from the king to use his ingenious device.

Soon enough, the gibbet rose in Halifax as a warning to thieves that the town no longer needed a hangman, or even an executioner. For this machine had a lead-weighted axe held aloft by means of a pin, and to the pin was attached a rope, and to the rope a beast. When the signal was given the animal was slapped and off it moved and out popped the pin. Down fell the axe and the sentence was swiftly served.

Sometimes the rope may have been passed among the crowd, who jointly pulled on it to release the pin, thereby deftly evading personal responsibility, and down fell the axe with its powerful impact on the victim's neck. Indeed, it was so powerful that there was once a gentlewoman passing by on her horse en route to the market; when the axe fell it sent the severed head flying into the air, over the heads of the spectators and into one of her panniers! Some, perhaps more inclined to raise the height of a good tale, say it fell into the lady's lap, where its teeth snapped shut on her apron and never more opened.

THE LUCK OF THE HEAD

Well they do say that a head will remain conscious for up to thirty minutes after it has been cut from the body, but whether it's true or not I couldn't tell you, and I'm not keen to find out. All I can tell you is that here in West Yorkshire is a town whose history revolves over and over around the image of the severed head, and in the seventeenth century, one of the most popular talismans for the houses of Halifax parish was the stone carving of a human head, pared down to its basic features. It was not so much a holy head for them; more a positively magical head capable of warding off all

sorts of misfortune. In the days before insurance companies you needed all the help you could get and people certainly seemed to believe in their power.

There was at least one case in West Yorkshire where a carved head seemed to make a positive difference, and that was at the Old Sun Inn at Haworth. Back in the early 1970s it was haunted, according to my friend Arthur. This wasn't some ordinary flitting, misty figure, though; this was a voice that would speak out of nowhere. Arthur was spoken to once himself in an empty tap-room one lunchtime. A sharp voice suddenly asked, 'What you a-doin' of theer?' Arthur said it nearly put him off his beer, but it was more of a worry for the landlord. The ghost – that's what they assumed it was, though they never actually saw anything – was heard often enough that the landlord feared it might damage trade, especially as he was planning to make it a dining sort of pub. After all, it might not be too good for your digestion, being spoken to like that. So he was asking his regulars what he could do and Arthur remembered something he'd come across at work.

Arthur worked for Bradford Museums Service and at that time in the early 1970s one of his colleagues, Sidney Jackson, was busy on a special project that he thought might establish an important line of continuity from the Iron Age to the present in West Yorkshire. From all around the Pennine fringe of the county he was coming across these curious carved stone heads, more like skulls than real people. Knowing that the Celts used to make heads like this, he first thought they were sculptures from that distant time and referred to them as Celtic heads. As time went on he realised that few, if any, were Celtic after all; most of them were probably from the last 200-300 years. Still, he'd drawn attention to these heads in the first place, and that was good, and he also discovered that people believed they kept misfortune away from a place, and that to do that they had to be placed at the threshold – over a door or window. And that's where you can still see lots of them, on medieval and nineteenth-century churches, seventeenth-century farmhouses and all sorts of other buildings, especially in the Calder and Aire valleys. They are still there doing their job, as they have for centuries.

So Arthur suggested that the landlord have one of these folksy, minimalist heads made and put up over the pub door. He did exactly that and it's been there since 1973. As far as Arthur knows, that voice hasn't been heard since and lots of people have enjoyed their dinner in peace. Though just lately its expression isn't as serene as it was, as a faux-traditional coaching lamp has been rather rudely stuck right in front of its nose. Not the best way to treat a head that's supposed to be looking out for you, I reckon.

Seven

A CIVIC BEAST

Another head that caused a stir in old West Yorkshire reminds us of a time when instead of mills and houses, or houses and cars, we had acres of forest, air clean enough for lichen to grow freely and places quiet enough not to put the beasts that lived in this green land on edge. It speaks of a time when there were animals roaming the hills that we no longer see here, and bands of men roaming those same hills in pursuit of these animals. Yorkshire still had its wild places and its wild beasts, and the wilder of these could be a problem for those who worked the fields and gathered nuts and wood from the forests.

THE GREAT BOAR OF BRADFORD

The head in this story also appears on the official insignia of a major town, bearing testimony to a founding legend. Just as Halifax today seems a far cry from the time when hermits lived there and pilgrims came in search of wonders, modern Bradford is not a place one associates with boars and hunters (or the gateway to fairyland, for that matter).

But boars were once at home all over Britain. They reckon the Vale of Pickering held one of the last wild herds in the 1200s, but with people like Henry III having 100 boars killed in 1251 for his Christmas feast, they obviously weren't likely to last long against such levels of consumption. After those days of medieval feasting, the only boars you got in Britain's forests were ones that had escaped from the parks of the gentry. There are various places claiming to be the location where the last wild boar was killed, like Shotover in Oxford and Wild Boar Fell in Cumbria. Whichever has the true claim, they each hold a vital memory of Britain's past.

However, there are some wild boar scattered around England again now, mostly in the south and west, thanks to more escapees, this time from more modern parks. There's even talk of reintroducing them properly as a native species. But we don't have so many forests nowadays, and boar need forests. One thing that did for them in the Middle Ages was the loss of the wildwood, another was the spread of human settlement. Any boar that managed to escape to the wild soon came into contact with people, and then there could be trouble. And that is how the story of how Bradford came to have a boar on its crest begins...

If you head out of Bradford towards Shipley, you go past Bradford Bank and Cliff Wood on your right. This was once a heavily wooded area, well used by locals for timber and, of course, for grazing a few pigs. Perhaps this was what attracted a large boar to the woods sometime in the fourteenth century. There weren't so many of his kind around by then, and surely a pig of any kind needs company. A boar with not just a sow but a farrow as well will be protective and rather aggressive – not always the best policy for an endangered species.

Also in those woods were a couple of well-known watering places; they're now called Spink Well and Boar's Well.

Now I remember at the Liverpool International Garden Festival in the 1980s that the weather was so hot that some pigs there had to be given some extra water. But they refused to drink the tap water they were given and in the end they had to be given bottled spring water. Obviously pigs are a bit picky about the water they drink, and that must be a recommendation for the wells of Cliff Wood. In fact, the water is so good that they later became a spa. You can visit them today, as the area around them has become an urban wildlife reserve and the wells have been made more accessible, but taking the waters is not recommended.

So with a supply of sows and sparkling springs, the boar called it home. The trouble was that he resented the intrusion of people upon his territory, and after he had killed some of them the locals began to avoid Cliff Wood. As it was a useful resource for the community there arose a cry that something had to be done, although preferably by someone else (nothing much changes) and so they petitioned their lord for assistance. The lord did what all good managers should do – he delegated. Or, more accurately, he subcontracted. The terms were clear: anyone who could kill the boar and bring proof of it (a severed head was always a popular way of proving something or someone was dead) would be granted land in Horton and gold to go with it.

Boar are elusive creatures, but it was well-known where this boar would go for refreshment. Finding the animal wouldn't be so hard for a man with patience. The hard part would be when it came to the killing, because boar are formidable when aroused. They have a tough hide and this particular boar had already shown that it had a fearsome temper, and was none too fond of people. So a hunter needed patience, courage and skill. It helped, too, to have an incentive, and the lord's offer of land provided just that.

John Rushworth heard the news and knew he had to act quickly. He wouldn't be the only one after the killer pig, and he wouldn't be the only one to hit on the simple scheme he planned to employ. He put on his protective leather gear, sharpened his sword and lance, packed his bow and quiver, called his dogs and set off for Cliff Wood.

He knew where he was headed: the watering spot where the boar had already been seen and had caused some mayhem. It was obviously a favourite spot and Rushworth knew that as long as he hid there and waited, his quarry would turn up sooner or later – if nobody else had already managed to kill the boar, that is.

Half the trick of getting people to call you brave is to use guile, and John Rushworth wasn't about to take unnecessary risks. So

when he found his luck was in and the boar emerged from the trees nearby, he set his dogs on it immediately. While his quarry was fending off the hounds, he attended to the animal from another angle. Before long, John Rushworth had blood on his gear and a dead boar at his feet, never more to sire progeny from the villagers' pigs, nor to terrify the local inhabitants.

The question now was how to take his trophy to the lord and claim his prize. Rushworth had no horse with him and the head of this beast was big and heavy; there was no way he could carry it to the lord's castle on foot. Yet he had to do something, he couldn't turn up at the lord's castle without some form of proof. Then he had a brainwave; he knelt down and cut out the boar's tongue with his dagger, carefully wrapped it up and stowed it in his bags. He washed his weapons, rinsed the blood off his clothes, called his dogs and set off walking.

A little while later another man rode into the clearing where the spring emerged, and was surprised as his horse suddenly baulked nervously. He looked and there he saw the body of this great boar lying in a pool of blood and a tumble of broken undergrowth near the spring. He quickly dismounted and checked the area round about. He couldn't understand it. He knew about the lord's offer, yet here was the boar, dead and with its head still attached. Perhaps it had been wounded elsewhere and had struggled here before dying. Perhaps the one who had administered the fatal blow was lying dead or injured somewhere. Or perhaps he who had killed it had forgotten to take the head, or was trusting that the body of the boar would stay there while he apprised the lord of his feat. Foolish! He took his chance and hacked off the boar's head, strapped it securely to his saddle and galloped off to see the lord about the promised land.

Well, in a race between a rider and a walker there's little doubt who has the advantage. Despite John Rushworth's head start, the rider arrived before him. He strode into the castle and sought an audience with the lord.

'I have killed the boar of Cliff Wood, sire, and I have the proof you require'. Attendants brought in the bloody head on a wooden board and the lord looked it over approvingly.

'Well done man, you have acquitted my challenge swiftly and admirably, and I suppose now you'd like your reward…' To this there was surely no answer but a deep bow. 'But first, tell me how you managed to put paid to this fine beast, for it was surely no easy task…' The false claimant had half-expected such a question, and began to tell his hastily-constructed tale.

While he was speaking, a servant ran into the hall and whispered in the lord's ear. The lord looked askance – there was another man claiming to have killed the boar, but here was the beast's head before him now! The lord saw a chance for a bit of fun; he would confront this new claimant with such compelling evidence as the severed head of the beast. Then he would amuse himself thinking

up some appropriate punishment for attempted fraud. He told his man to let the newcomer in.

John Rushworth, still dusty from the road, strode into the hall, but stopped dead when he saw the boar's head lying there. He looked at the head, at the lord, at the man standing proudly, even smugly, over the head, and he swiftly took in the situation. He had, after all, taken steps for such an eventuality.

'Lord, I submit to you that I have killed the boar that raged in Cliff Wood with my own hands, and I believe I have proof, if you will allow me...'

'Better proof than its head, is it?' The lord was understandably doubtful.

'I believe you may think it so, my lord.' The other claimant began to feel nervous, wondering if his lies were about to be discovered.

Rushworth was already reaching into the pack he had with him, and he brought out a small package. Unwrapping it carefully, he produced a bloody object and knelt by the boar's head. He prised open the animal's maw and invited the lord to look inside.

'Lord, I have no horse and I could not carry the head. If I had tried I would have been vulnerable to thieves, so I cut out the

beast's tongue. Here, I have brought it to you. This tongue may tell you who truly killed this fine beast. If you doubt my story, you might perhaps ask this man how his boar's head came to lose its tongue on the way here.'

The other man shifted uneasily. His expectations of land and an improved life had vanished, to be replaced by an expectation of something far less welcome. The lord ordered his men to take him aside until he was ready to speak with him, and that is the last we hear of the false claimant in the tale.

Rushworth, meanwhile, was congratulated by the lord not only for his job well done, but also for his shrewdness in selecting the tongue as proof of his endeavours. 'Perhaps it is that shrewdness as much as your bravery that qualifies you to receive this gift of land, Rushworth, but to keep it in your family you will have to perform a ceremony to maintain your tenure.'

The details were set out, the agreements reached, the conditions of maintenance agreed and Rushworth left the hall that day the new holder of lands in Horton. There were around fifteen or twenty acres in all, two parcels of land that came to be known as Hornblow and Hunt Yard. With them came a horn and the requirement to turn up at Bradford Marketplace at Martinmas each year with the horn and his dog. There, Rushworth or his descendants would hold the dog and proclaim to the assembled crowds 'Heirs of Rushworth come, hold my hound while I blow three blasts of my horn to pay my rent due to my sovereign lord the king'. Which was not too onerous a service for a parcel of land.

Well, all that was around 600 years ago, they say, and later the inn known as the Robin Hood & Little John was built on the land. The inn was pulled down in about 1800 after nearly 200 years on the spot. And for much of that time the horn, which they now call the Gelder's Horn, was preserved and used at the commencement of Bradford's great market. It is over 2ft feet long, dappled green in colour and it is still kept in the City Hall as a relic from Bradford's past. The official insignia of the city tells the story again every time it appears for those who know the significance of the boar's head without a tongue and the pair of hunting horns. You'll even see the boar's head on some of the badges of the Bantams, Bradford City FC!

Eight

ROBIN AGAIN

At the end of the story of the Bradford boar, we find another reference to Robin Hood in the name of the inn. Maybe the establishment once bore a traditional rhyme for such inns, such as that which can still be seen over the doorway of the Robin Hood Inn at Pecket Well: 'If Robin Hood be not at home, come take a pot with Little John'. Nonetheless, with the inn's connection to the hunting of Bradford's fearsome boar, it seems to return us to the nature of Robin as hunter, rather than outlaw. But then, 'Many speak of Robin as never drew his bow', as the local saying goes, and that goes for most of us who tell his stories. But should that stop us? By no means!

Of course, ask most people around the world and they'll tell you Robin was a Nottingham man, and a denizen of Sherwood Forest. But ask someone from Yorkshire, especially one who's read the ballads, and you'll be told that's not necessarily the case. Read the early ballads yourself and you might agree with them, for here you'll find yourself roaming the lands of Barnsdale which stretched from the River Don, around Sheffield, to the River Aire which flows through Leeds. That's West Riding territory and there's good reason to claim Robin as a Yorkshire figure. But to my mind, anyone who tries to pin Robin down as this or that person in history, born at this or that place and with this or that personal biography, may have caught something of Robin's history at the expense of a broader understanding of the legends.

Can it be any real man who stood at Blackstone Edge, by Robin Hood's Bed, and tossed a great stone six miles into Lancashire? And left that stone, still to be seen at Monstone Edge, with the imprint of his thumb and finger? Can it be a real man who threw two great boulders across the Calder Valley while playing pennystone, an old working-man's form of quoits? One of Robin Hood's pennystones can still be seen on Midgley Moor, embedded in the ground. If he was a real man he was big; big enough to stride the 60ft or so between the pinnacles of Robin Hood's Stride in the Peak District, and big enough to send arrows flying for miles, like at Whitby and at Alwalton, near Peterborough. But his most famous arrow flight was surely his last one, and that one was smack in the middle of West Yorkshire.

THE DEATH OF ROBIN HOOD

One thing the old balladeers agreed on is that if they told of Robin's death, they placed it at Kirklees Priory, between Huddersfield and Dewsbury, and they told it something like this…

Robin and his gang of followers were outlaws and would have lived like guerrillas. If they had homes and families they would have spent little time with them, as it would have been dangerous for all involved. Their abode would have been the outdoors – traditionally the forest where concealment is easier – and their means of sustenance would have been whatever they could glean from their environment. It sounds, in story form, terribly romantic to live in the greenwood, to hunt and gather your food and harass the arrogant officials of Church and State; but the truth is that life could be hard. This was especially so in winter, when the cold and damp would seep into your bones, the firewood was damp and slow to blaze, and the hunting and gathering provided sparse fare. By spring, the blood would be running slow and the spirit hard to rouse. The aches would have been around just too long, and the time would be ripe for some kind of physical overhaul. We would say it's time for a detox, but back then, maybe six

centuries ago or more, the remedy was to run off a little of the old, thick and sluggish blood.

Robin had been living his outlaw's life for twenty-two years, and all those years were surely beginning to tell on him. So one spring he announced to his followers that he was going to take a couple of days away to visit his cousin, Elizabeth. She was Prioress at Kirklees and skilled in medicine.

His men were not too happy with this idea and protested. To them, visiting a lady who had a high position in the Church – whose officials they had regularly targeted – was dangerous enough, but it was also common knowledge that she had a close association with a man who could be even more of a threat to Robin. Several of them wanted to go with him, well-armed for security, and Will Scarlett was especially vehement.

'Master, this winter must have dulled your wits! You have surely heard the rumours of the Prioress and her dalliance with Roger of Doncaster. We have lightened his panniers on many occasions and he lives close by the priory. He is not a man to cross lightly. If you intend to go that way, you need fifty bowmen at least.'

'What are you thinking, Will? This is a priory, a refuge for holy women, and it is not for the likes of bands of men like us! We should attract too much attention, put too great a strain on their hospitality and tax the affections of the local people. I shall go with Little John and he shall be my companion, for it is near where we first met, at Clifton.'

'Robin, listen to me, for God's sake – we are all uneasy about this plan of yours, and can you be sure of where her affections most closely lie…?'

'Leave it, Will! Neither should we blacken the reputations of the good women of Kirklees, especially my kinswoman. I am too tired for an argument like this. I shall go to the Prioress, who is family and surely means no harm to myself. She shall draw off a little of my blood and I shall recover some of my vigour for the spring. Then when we come back we may resume our little adventures. But for now, just leave it. Little John shall be my only companion.'

And off they went, the two of them, leaving dissent and unease behind them. They headed towards the hills overlooking the River Calder, where the priory and its grounds stood. By nightfall they came to a stream with a plank bridge across it, and upon this bridge knelt an old lady, crying and muttering. As they came closer, they could hear her words; a crazy mixture of invective and lament, cursing Robin Hood for leaving his friends with harsh words between them and bewailing that this headstrong act would cause his downfall.

'Why do you lament thus, old woman?' asked Robin.

'Because his bones are old, and his wits are slow, but his pride is hard and fast to rise. And rather than listen to sound advice, he ignores his friends who better know, and by that he is sold.'

'And why should that be?'

'He goes to be bled by his own near kin, but shall never pass this way again.'

'You speak ill of my kin, old woman, as my companions did before. And so like them, I hold your words of no matter. I know full well my cousin would never seek my harm, and you will have no need to weep for me'. Then, remembering his manners, 'I trust we shall meet again on my return.'

And on they went, a little quiet and chastened by this odd encounter, till they came to the Priory. Outside the nunnery was the hospital and guest house, but it was not there that Robin went. He knocked at the gatehouse and asked for the Prioress. When he had explained his errand, she took him into a small room on the first floor where there was a single pallet bed.

They chatted about family matters and about their lives, and the Prioress chided him about his frequent harassment of bishops and other churchmen travelling on the highways. 'Ah', Robin said in good humour, and explained once more the code of conduct he and his men observed. 'You surely know, cousin, that those that are honest and true, they pass by without harm, and sometimes even pass well fed by us. But those who have grown fat and wealthy from their office, acquiring their wealth by the sweat of others' brows, they must sometimes pay a toll on their life's highway. Outlaws we may be, but we have many friends among the people who know we pose no threat to honest folk. Why, without us some might never have tasted good venison! And certainly their bellies would be emptier. Is this not a true Christian service?' And he gave her £20 for the upkeep of the Priory.

'It should stop, Robin, it should have stopped long ago, for your luck is not without limit', but she knew that, without pardon, it could never stop, and with her cousin's pride it never would. 'Any man who does not take due heed of warning, Robin, I deem unwise indeed.'

And she pulled up Robin's sleeve and affixed the needle of the letting-iron into a vein on the inside of his arm. Robin grunted and lay back as the treatment began. A trickle of blood began to run down the channel into a bowl beside him. Elizabeth laid a hand on his arm, 'Now lay there, Robin, and relax, and I shall be back in a while to remove the irons.'

Robin had been bled often before and while his blood dripped into the bowl beside him he lay on the bed and daydreamed, and he began to doze. And first the blood ran thick, and then it began to run thin. Robin, waking from his weary slumber, realised that treason was within.

John, meanwhile, was lounging outside the gatehouse, wondering why it was all taking so long, when he heard Robin's horn

blow. But this was not the lusty sound of a man restored to vitality, it was little more than the despairing cry of a wounded beast. He rushed into the gatehouse and up the stairs into the treatment room. He saw the bowl brimming over with his friend's blood, he saw the ghastly pallor of Robin's face, and he took in the situation immediately.

'Robin, you've been betrayed, just as Will warned!' he raged. 'We shall come to this foul house and burn down this treacherous nunnery for this deed!' But Robin held up his hand.

'John, you know I swore never to harm a woman and it would do me no good with Our Lord if I were to break my vow on my deathbed. God knows, it is my pride that has led me to this and now I must answer to Him for it.' Robin, leaning weakly against the wall, looked through the window towards the woods and sighed.

'Ah, poor, good Will… John, fix an arrow and hand me my bow, will you? There can be no burial for me in hallowed ground, so fate can choose my final resting place. I leave you, John, if you will, to be my bearer.'

Robin pulled back the bowstring and it pained John to see how little the bow bent, to hear how much deeper than usual was the sound of the string snapping back as the arrow sped forth. Yet still that arrow flew more than 500yds and where it landed, there Little John bore the body, dug the grave and laid Robin by the old highway. In later days, Little John made light of it and talked up his friend's legendary strength.

'Robin let off three arrows', he'd say. 'The first one landed at Haigh Cross and that's five miles away, and I told him "I'm not carrying you there, master, you're still a big chap even if you're smaller than me", and I told him to shoot another one. That one landed in the River Calder! "How do you expect me to bury you in a river, Robin?" I said, "Shoot another!" And that's how he ended up on the edge of the Priory, where the nuns could never forget him.'

On that spot, years later, people would still stop and remember Robin Hood and his exploits. Though his gravestone was moved and though it had false epitaphs engraved upon it, people still

remembered his death by treachery at the hands of his kinswoman, the Prioress of Kirklees.

Little John's plea for the destruction of the nunnery, refused by Robin, was at last realised in 1539 by King Henry VIII – and perhaps the king's pretext was not so different from Robin Hood's. He too deplored the riches of the Roman Catholic Church, after all, though it was towards the relatively cash-poor English State that he diverted its fortunes.

Today, just a gatehouse remains above ground to show where Kirklees Priory stood. Although it was built after the first legends of Robin's death appeared, stories tell of a figure believed to be Robin at the upstairs window, and of spectral arrows flying through the air. Some people have seen a female figure roaming the grounds of the old nunnery, which they believe is the tormented and restless spirit of his treacherous kinswoman. Robin's grave still stands secluded in a wooded grove, its remains enclosed by the rusted fragments of an iron cage erected over it to protect the stone from predation – for it was said that a piece chipped from Robin Hood's tombstone, placed under the pillow, would cure toothache. But is it a grave? For when the earth beneath was investigated long ago, no body was found…

Nine

A TRUST BETRAYED

Everybody knows of Robin Hood and of Marian, the woman he loved. At one time she was a maid, but surely not for long in her association with the hero of the greenwood. Robin and Marian are often spoken of in the same breath, but in truth it seems they didn't meet until nearly 1500! Moreover, it was not in one of the traditional ballads that they met but, more fittingly perhaps, at the games that were held every May in Tudor times. Robin became Lord of the May, and a good Lord of the May needed a suitable consort – not a coy maid, but a knowing woman at home with the innuendo and ribaldry of an old-style village fête. Robin had met his match and their fame spread into later centuries, into the tales we tell today. Theirs is a love story that apparently ends happily – sadly, not always the case in our West Yorkshire legends.

FAIR BECCA

Rebecca and her sweetheart had been seeing each other on an increasingly intimate basis for several months and, truth to tell, it was one of the few things that brightened up the young woman's life, living as she did on the moor edge at Baildon. Her lover was a good-looking young man and always dressed well, whatever they were planning to get up to when they met. Well, she thought, that's what befits a young man from a good family like his must be. Although sometimes she idly wondered what a young man with a good education and assured income saw in a bog-edger like herself – apart from certain obvious charms, of course – she more often daydreamed of other possibilities.

Bright and optimistic though she was, Becca's future had never seemed to her to hold much hope of anything but hard work unless she could attract a good marriage. She was an only child and would inevitably inherit the farm, but their land was no great prize and her family could not offer a substantial dowry. The most she had to offer was her good looks and folk in the countryside around seemed to agree that she had those in abundance – which is why everybody called her Fair Becca.

So in those too-short hours when they would slip away to some quiet spot, romance and passion ruled, and anything seemed possible. Loving thoughts were expressed while they lay back and watched the clouds, and Becca began to imagine a fine new set of fire-irons being put in her hands as a sign that she was the mistress of domestic affairs in a bigger house not so far away, where the food would be plentiful and varied and she might even be able to support her parents in their old age.

Her lover, Tom, equally smitten with Becca and hardly caring for the social gap between them as they lay on the ground, did nothing to dispel such dreams. 'How wonderful to be like this forever', he sighed, 'Oh, if I could carry you off with me…' In such moments Becca had neither reason nor will to doubt his sincerity and perhaps nor should we.

But times were different then and in affairs of the heart, the heart did not always prevail. Class, family, status, money, self-improvement – all these had their say and love came well down the frame. Many a woman chosen by a man's heart, and vice versa, held hopes that the other's family would dash. What Becca didn't know was that Tom's family had picked out another woman for him. It was a familiar story: Becca had the most of his love and Tom's family tolerated her as a young bachelor's natural whim, but their choice offered better prospects socially and financially.

There was no contest. If Tom didn't marry his family's candidate he could say goodbye to his financial security. It was not a decision he wanted to make, but it was one that was to be pushed on him by circumstances. His father commiserated, 'Aye, Tom, she's a fair lass and if I were younger my own eyes'd be turned, I can tell ye! But I wish she weren't so local, like. My father used to warn me not to wipe my mucky boots on my own doorstep, and it was he who fixed me up with your mother in the end. So take care, lad, and remember you'll be marrying into a good future next spring.'

The better-connected girl doesn't really feature in our tale, of course, but we can imagine that she too was aware that her impending alliance was more of a family affair than a love affair. However, we have no idea what she felt about Tom, and we don't even know her name – so let's call her Alice for this story.

What we do know is that Thomas and Becca were getting on very well, and despite his father's warning they were getting rather carried away. Indeed, Becca was anticipating his proposal, which was perhaps why they allowed themselves to get rather too carried away in those welcoming fields. One day, when Tom ran up to surprise Becca where she was working, he found her anxious. She confided that her time was late and she feared the worst. Well, the shock of this news somehow reminded Tom of Alice, but he knew full well that a man must do 'the right thing' and deal with his own mistakes. So he took a deep breath, smiled and said, 'Then, Becca, we must get you married!' Becca sighed and held him, and once more they made love. But Tom found his thoughts wandering – to Alice, to his father, to his future. A few hours later he returned home, deep in thought, and spoke to his father about his predicament. It was no longer time for fatherly advice, though.

'Son, I very much regret your news, but I must remind you that you are already spoken for. You say that you are more drawn to Becca, but what are her prospects? What are your prospects? We have already talked of this. The country hereabouts already expects you to marry Alice, and if you should not then we would very much fall out of favour both of her family and her peers. No marriage to Becca will recover that favour. I cannot support it, Tom, and baby or not you shall have to tell her so.'

Well, this of course just made things harder for Tom. He could marry Becca and they would be left precarious, with a child; or he could reject her, and they would still lose their honour when their child was born. There was no easy way out – shame and dishonour were, he could see, inevitable, unless circumstances could be encouraged to turn out otherwise.

So three days after he had last seen her, Tom rode up to Becca. He had a full pannier on his horse, and he patted it. 'My beautiful Becca,' he said 'I have here some bridal things that will suit you well I think, and if you will, perhaps you would accompany me to church at Wilsden'. Did Rebecca notice that he seemed to lack some of his usual gaiety? Did she notice and attribute it to the importance of his decision? Or was she caught up in the moment of anticipation? That night, after all, she would be married and sharing a bed rather than bracken! Eyes shining, she jumped up on his horse, wrapped her arms around his waist and laid her head against his back. Off they went across the hill.

Tom was uncharacteristically quiet as they rode, but her heart leapt when he turned off the road towards Old Allen Pits. They'd spent many a happy hour alone here together, and it may even have been one of those hours that had got her into her present state. 'Oh Tom,' she murmured 'is this some kind of romantic detour? What time must we be at church?'

'Oh, you needn't worry about that, Becca', he said.

They rode as they usually did to the farthest of the old coal pits, where they were least likely to be seen. Becca's heart was beating faster as they dismounted.

'Fair Becca, you are so beautiful', he said, appraising her as she stood, her bump beginning to show. He laid his hand tenderly on her stomach. She sank into his arms and he held her very tight. 'Becca, we have to get you dressed in your bridals, but first you must take off your everyday things.' And not for the first time here at the old pits, she undressed before him. His heart beat more

strongly, for she was beautiful and she was ready to be his entirely – only of course it could not be. His options were exhausted. He got back on his horse and looked down at her astonished face. He spoke formally, firmly.

'Rebecca, our wedding cannot be. My father will not support me unless I marry another. And if we have no money to support us, then our unhappiness will be assured. I cannot bear to think of you dishonoured by a child and abandonment. There is only one way.'

With that he spurred his horse and rode hard at the young woman. Becca screamed and ran across the heath, but Tom pursued her for each turn she made, forcing her closer and closer to one of the old pits, then around and around the edge of the pit, until she stopped on the bank of loose spoil ringing its mouth. Tom sidled the horse closer, until she finally slipped and fell headlong into the old workings.

Her scream stopped suddenly, but there was still movement below. Tom dismounted and came to the edge of the pit. He could hear moaning. 'Becca, my love', he called. 'Forgive me, it must be for the best – but believe me, it breaks my heart.'

And she gasped weakly from the dark depths, 'It breaks my heart too, Tom – but this breaks my body also, as you planned. But I shall never leave you Tom, believe this. Look for me where we enjoyed our love together, for while the holly grows green, I swear to you that I shall come again and again until the end of my allotted span'.

And there fell a silence between them which was never again broken. Tom collected her clothing and threw it down the pit after her. As an afterthought, he threw the bridal dress down too, for if things had been different, could have been different, surely she would have been the one to wear it at his side. He sighed. Strange, he thought, he should have been relieved at taking a step to solve his problems, but all he felt was loss beyond all he could imagine when he was hatching his scheme. He rode home slowly.

'Have you told her then, lad?' asked his father as he arrived.

'Yes, Father. I'm afraid she took it rather badly. As do I, I confess.'

'That's to be expected, son. But a bit of gold in the purse usually helps us all get used to things, and you'll do well enough with Alice. What did Rebecca say?'

'She said she'd never leave me. She may be right.'

'I'm sorry, lad, but it'll pass, though I'm sure it doesn't feel like it. Believe me, your future is brighter this way.'

Tom looked at his father, sighed, and went out. He left his horse in the stable and he walked all the way to Horton. Night had fallen and more than once he fancied he saw a flash of white, like the swirl of a shirt, lighten the shadows. He walked on, his heart growing heavier, and came to an inn. There he took supper and a drink. A few drinks, indeed, and he sat there with his head in his hands, occasionally getting up and pacing the room. The other drinkers grew curious. One bought him a drink and came and sat at his table.

'Cum, lad, you look a fair misery. Mebbe it'd be easier to talk about it, eh? Share a trouble, bear a trouble, as we say.'

'There's no bearing this trouble, friend'. But the man sat, determined to hear Tom's story, whatever it may be, for his friends back at the bar, and he asked a few shrewd questions.

'It's a girl, ennit? Aye, it's only ever bin a girl who's got me to looking like you do now. Why, d' ye knaw, I lost me dog a year or two back, and I'd 'ad 'im for nigh twelve year, and he were always a good worker, and good for the rabbits an' all, and I were right down in t' mouth when 'e died. But it were nothing to when my Jennie went off wi' ol' Bully from o'er Otley way, I were in a reight state, drinking an' all, just like you. And I'd only 'ad 'er two years, mind! These women can get ter yer, sure enough.'

So at length, Tom told his story. He told of how he'd loved Rebecca, how he'd had to throw her over for another because of his father's objection, how he'd walked with her to the place they'd spent many a happy hour together and how he'd told her there how things stood, and how unhappy she'd been, how unhappy they'd both been, how she'd threatened to do herself in and how he'd had to turn away and leave her there, he was weeping so hard. 'And you know what she said?' he asked his new friend. 'She said

she'd never leave me as long as the holly grew green. She'll be with me till the end of my days, I know.'

'Nah then, lad, it'll pass', and they talked a little more until the man rejoined his friends. 'Seems like just another broken heart, but there were one funny thing 'e said. 'E said as 'ow 'er last words were that she'd never leave him while th' holly grows green. Now, is that a promise or a curse?'

Suspicions were raised simply enough in those days and after Tom had finally set off home the fellows in the pub discussed the matter. The next day, the news spread from Baildon that a young girl was missing from her home, and they felt that they should check out the young man's story.

So some of them walked up to Old Allen Pits, where the lad said he and his sweetheart had gone, and they found a set of hoof prints leading off the road. They followed the trail to the furthest of the workings and in a secluded hollow they found the earth churned up, as if by someone riding a horse hard. The trail then followed a crazy route towards the pits, and someone found the imprint of a foot, a bare foot, in the mud, and then another. These tracks went as far as one of the old pits and stopped. 'He said they'd walked – but we've hoof prints in a bit of a lather here and some bare feet, a girl's by the looks of it. Mebbe better take a look down this 'ere 'oil, I'd say.'

Of course, at the foot they found young Rebecca in her underclothes, and the jumble of clothes tumbled across her. Bloody and cold she was, and bloody and cold she was brought out of that pit and taken to the nearest inn for the inquest. All things being considered, the Constable decided he needed to talk to Thomas, and though for a while Tom insisted she must have done away with herself in the mine after he'd abandoned her, he began to crack when the Constable produced a sprig of holly from his bag. 'She said something about holly, sir, I believe…'

So it was justice, not love, that finally decided Tom's future and Alice married another. But for years after, people walking near the old pits and in Hollingworth Lane and Hew Clews, were startled on moonlit nights by the apparition of something white, like a woman in a bridal gown, drifting around. They remembered Fair Becca; remembered her so well that her old home became known as Fair Becca Farm. But after a while, some say round about 1899, her shade was no longer seen – some folk reckoned she had been frightened off by all the new mills, but the older folk said Rebecca would've reached the end of what would have been her natural life, for a soul even if prematurely interrupted in its preordained journey cannot leave this world till its time is done.

Ten

A Dog's Life

Once upon a time in some parts of West Yorkshire, a young man or maid would try and catch a snail by its horns and toss it over their left shoulder. No fun for the snail perhaps, but if they could manage this small feat then the path of true love would be smoother. Not that it's easy to grab a snail's horns, and that surely is a measure of the expectation of love running smoothly.

England's Civil War, when friends, neighbours and even family members fought each other in their own land, was surely a war that broke more hearts in this country than most. Loyalties could switch according to opportunity and astuteness, and sometimes love itself might be caught in between.

Except where there were obligations involved, of course, there was a certain class element present in the decision over which side to take, just as there were class factors involved in one's choice of spouse. However, as any Jane Austen reader knows, things can get a lot more complicated than class, and much might come down to whether the desired spouse's family actually liked you.

The Canine Messenger

A young cavalier who lived at Toothill in Rastrick met this kind of unexpected and unwelcome opposition. He had been seeing a young woman from a good home, Newhouse Hall in Sheepridge, near Huddersfield. A great deal of mutual affection had certainly grown up between the young man and Sybil, as she was called.

Their meetings were almost brought to a halt, however, by Sybil's father. He was a staunch Royalist himself and very clear on how things should be in society. Inevitably, he was a strict sort at home and very particular about whom his daughter would marry. After all, in those turbulent days whoever won her hand might also lay a claim on some of his own fortune, so you couldn't be too careful. And something about this young man set him on edge – he didn't like him, and he didn't want him in his family. 'Sybil,' he declared, 'this young man does not seem to me as steadfast as you might wish in a husband, and I would counsel you against pursuing your affections in this direction.'

Good counsel rarely stopped a heart beating, though, and the uncertainties of Civil War brought about a hardening of the old man's resolve. This was a time, he thought, when you needed to be sure of those around you, and while the world was being turned upside down, class was surely no longer a reliable guide to character. He spoke to his daughter again to make his feelings perfectly plain and, he thought, final.

'Sibyl,' he said, 'I have counselled you against this man before, yet you continue to meet him and to invite him to my house. I say to you now that the next time he comes here you are to tell him that you can never meet or communicate again and he is no longer to entertain any thoughts of a closer association with this family. You can also tell him he is no longer welcome here. Indeed, I shall tell him myself when I see him'. And he did, in terms that left the young man feeling altogether rather bitter. Sybil herself was feeling wretched, but had no choice but to go along with her father's wishes – or appear to.

The frustrated lovers wrung their hands and their hearts at their unhappy fate but, as they say, necessity will find a way. The young man had a dog, a sociable spaniel, who knew the hall and was very friendly with Sybil. So, when occasion allowed, it would be sent off over the fields to call at the hall itself, bearing a message from the

young man to his lady friend. She in turn would fuss over it just long enough to take the message and send her own back. It was by no means a perfect arrangement, but it worked, after a fashion, to keep their love alive.

A regular visiting hound does tend to arouse suspicions, though, and Sybil's father shortly guessed something was going on. He lingered in Felgreave Wood one day, waiting for the dog to pass on its errand of heart's-ease, and the animal's friendliness was its undoing. Seeing a familiar face, it interrupted its journey and came wagging its tail towards the old man, never expecting the sword that suddenly and cruelly came down upon its neck, severing its head instantly. However, galvanised by shock, the body of the poor animal turned tail and ran off through the wood towards its home, leaving the old man to pick up its head and the letter that fell from the now-empty collar.

This was, as we can imagine, a very unpleasant surprise for Sybil later that day; and no more pleasant was the surprise that awaited the young man when he came across the headless body of his favourite dog, with a trail of blood leading back into the depths of Felgreave Wood. Whether it would have done them any good to toss a snail or not, these two young people could scarcely have met a rougher path for their affections. So what became of the characters in this tragic drama?

It seems that neither of the two lovers got over the shock of that vengeful day. Poor Sybil pined and eventually pined away; while the young man, appalled at the whole thing, switched sides and joined the Parliamentary cause, arrayed against Sybil's father and all he stood for. Perhaps the old man thought to himself, 'Ah-ha! A turncoat, just as I expected', and perhaps he wished he could tell his daughter that he had been right all along. Or perhaps he just wondered if he had really been right, after all.

As for the dog, it remained as a silent witness, a messenger to future generations, as it was still to be seen streaking headless through Felgreave Wood, a bane to anyone who sees him.

Eleven

A YORKSHIRE
TRAGEDY

They say there's a little bit of truth in every legend, though there's a good bit of story too. Often there's also a bit of legend in any dramatic episode of history. It all depends on who's telling the story, of course.

Take ghosts, for instance. People always want to believe it's an actual being behind a haunting, someone who's had a bit of tragedy in their lives and can't let it go, or maybe one of those unfortunate souls who contrive to create their own disaster for the rest of us to wonder at, like an old drama on television, endlessly replayed for our questionable entertainment. The characters go on revisiting the scene time and again, and sometimes one of us catches sight of them.

Maybe they want us to – maybe they want us to say, 'Look, it's OK, you don't need to keep doing this, it's time to move on and do whatever dead people do. Maybe there's a better place and maybe you need to come back and try again, but what you're doing now isn't getting anyone anywhere.'

Maybe there are some of us who might be able to help these visitors from another region of reality to move on. But mostly when we see what we think must be a ghost, we feel a bit flustered and a bit puzzled, because our brains are working overtime trying to work out whether this fits into our normal of perception – that's if it's a gentle or quiet sort of spirit. If it isn't, then we're more likely to be just plain scared.

One way to try and explain such a disquieting experience is to relate it to some known local incident. However, then history begins to change to make way for the legend, and sometimes it's hard to disentangle fact from fancy.

WALTER LOSES IT

Plain scared would have been most people's reaction to old Walter's ghost, up at the hall in Calverley. This was with good reason, because Walter Calverley, apparently not a man of 'sober behaviour' in his last years became, on 23 April 1605, a thorough monster. After that no one had any doubt as to who was responsible for the fearful noises and ghastly apparitions around his old home.

But surely Walter is a historical figure, not a folk tale? I would agree, had I not come across various divergent accounts of this episode. If the facts don't agree, then surely someone is telling a story. The question is, who?

Well, that's a question for the historians amongst you. As far as I could glean, Walter Calverley seems to have been a reasonably pleasant young man, brought up in a good family in a fine stone-clad hall in the village that gave the family their name. Somewhat passionate and single-minded, it was said he switched his affections from one young lady so abruptly that she pined away. If only she'd known what was to become of him and the woman for whom she had been jilted, maybe she would have felt a bit more positive about the outcome. It was also said that he was lucky not to have been caught up in the Guy Fawkes affair – his family were staunch Roman Catholics and some of the conspirators would have been in the family's social circle and around Walter's age. Passionate though he was, Walter and his family came through unscathed.

The woman he finally married was Philippa, a suitable young lady from a good family and with ample wealth. Yet they ran into difficulties when, after some time, no child had been forthcoming from their union. No child meant no heir; no heir spelt an end to the family line and disgrace for the failed progenitor. Walter, a man of his time and indeed, some might say, a man of his time too much of the time, came to assume she was barren and the marriage was without hope, and he didn't take it at all well. He was not inclined to think that he might be responsible for this state of affairs; but it must have occurred to him, which couldn't have helped. Either way, from his point of view things looked bleak. By all accounts that was when he found that a drink or two helped push his anxieties away for a while.

Walter and his wife had a friend by the name of Leventhorp, who got on very well with Philippa. She was evidently well taken with him as he became a frequent visitor to the hall. We don't know quite how well these two got on, and there is no talk in the accounts of them constructing an illicit relationship, but the mood in the household lightened. Then at last a child was born – a boy and an heir to the Calverley name and property.

There was, naturally, much relief and rejoicing, and then soon after came the first stirrings of another child! This one too went to term and was another boy. Surely now the family could relax; it would be a severe tragedy indeed that would lead to loss of the Calverley inheritance.

However, even in the celebrations everyone must have wondered why the years of barrenness had suddenly given way to such a productive period; even more so when Philippa fell pregnant a third time.

Walter should have been happy of course, but he was not entirely sure. He reflected that his wife's fecundity had begun a year or so after Leventhorp had come into the family's life, and even at that time, watching their amiable chatter, he had felt suspicious. With the passage of time and the arrival of two more children, the suspicion did not diminish in the slightest. He again found a drink or two would ease his anxieties and help him to think. Before long he came to conclude that the children were not actually his progeny but Leventhorp's, and that he needed to make his feelings known about the matter. It didn't help at all that his fortunes were suffering from the years of excess, and a bigger family naturally entailed bigger outgoings.

The birth of the third child in 1604 therefore came at a bad time, and brought things to a head. Walter finally snapped and confronted his wife. Philippa was still weak from a difficult delivery and the scene grew heated and distressing. Walter finally stormed downstairs and distracted himself in the usual manner until, after an evening of raving and cursing, he fell asleep where he lay.

He didn't feel any better the next morning, and at this point his younger brother arrived at his door in search of financial assistance for his university studies. A quick look at his own accounts persuaded Walter how dire his position was and everything rushed in upon him. There he was being cuckolded, he was sure, and even if he wasn't, his way of life had compromised the future for himself and his whole family. Things were unravelling fast, not only in the Calverley household but in Walter's mind. He contemplated his dagger – perhaps that was the most painless way out for all of them, he thought.

Well, I must say the different accounts I've read tend to disagree as to Walter's early life and character, as well as the actual possibility of an affair and the cause of Walter's despair; but at this stage they all tend to come together for the final act.

Walter sank quickly into a frenzy of despair, and as he sat in the hall-body in this volatile state of mind, his eldest son ran in. Perhaps the lad, who was just four years old, mithered him, but whatever the spur, his father lashed out and stabbed his son several times. After this enormity, there was only one way forward and he carried the news, in the form of the bleeding child, to the room where his wife sat and their second son was playing.

'Here' he said 'is the reward for your dalliance and my madness'. As he said this, he threw the child to the floor, freeing his knife hand for his second son, thrusting the dagger through his heart. Philippa rushed forward screaming, but met the point of the

dagger herself as Walter struck again. Luckily, she was wearing a steel-framed girdle that kept her from fatal injury – though Walter didn't realise it. He was off out the door, throwing a servant down the stairs in the process.

Walter apparently assumed his business was done in that house as he rushed out, jumped on his horse and rode furiously away. He had one destination in mind – the house where his third child would be found. This child, along with the tension that was building up in the house, had taken it out of Philippa and for her sake the baby, Henry, had been sent out to a wet nurse. So that was where Walter was headed, in all haste and presumably with a similar design. But perhaps he rode a little too furiously, a little too roughly on his mount, as for some reason the horse reared as they rode through Calverley

Woods. Walter found himself tumbling through the air until the hard ground took the wind out of him. This was the opportunity for the family servants in pursuit to jump on their maddened master and subdue him, and Calverley's mayhem was finally over.

So the third child went unharmed; but back at the hall there were two children dead and a woman and servant injured, and there was no doubt over the one responsible. Walter was taken away and put in confinement. Upon examination he freely confessed and claimed he acted because he was sure the children were not his, and that his wife had been unfaithful. He had been considering such an action for four years, he said, since his wife's first pregnancy, but something about that third baby must have set him off.

The countryside was abuzz with news of the tragedy and gossip over Walter's way of life and undoing. But by the time of his trial he was sober, remorseful and determined to preserve his family's inheritance, which would be at threat if he pleaded guilty of murder.

So Walter Calverley finally did the right thing and refused to plead. He could not in all conscience plead not guilty, and a guilty plea would put his surviving family at risk of his property being forfeited to the Crown, so he stood firm before the court. He was warned that justice required him to declare one way or the other, and that refusal to do so laid him open to a particularly unpleasant form of judicial persuasion – the *peine forte et dure*, or 'strong, intense pain'.

Still Walter remained resolute, so he was led off and laid between two wooden boards with a stone under his back and his hand held by one of his servants. One by one, weights were placed on the top board, straining his back over the stone, yet Walter's will still did not crack – unlike his back and ribcage as he was slowly crushed to death. Eventually, Walter's grip on his servant's hand slackened as death mercifully arrived. His estate survived to be inherited by his third and now only son. And Philippa? Well, she did not marry a Leventhorp, that we know.

If the locals were aghast at his previous doings, they were no less so as news came of his stoic resistance to the torture. Such a man, such events – good or bad – leave a wake in the stream of history, and for many years after, the locals were convinced that Walter Calverley was still in their midst.

Some told tales of a man riding a headless horse in the lanes around the village and through Calverley Woods; or of a mist enveloping them as they entered the woods, gradually taking human form and keeping pace with them as they passed through. Others spoke of his spectre, its features twisted in frenzy and rage, wafting purposefully down a corridor at the hall – at least until the corridor was bricked up, like the door to the murder bedroom. It was said that the wraiths of the wood would disappear into a cave among the trees, so they sent ministers and cunning men to try and lay old Walter, but he resisted their entreaties just as he had resisted those of the judges, and rode on until at last one man managed to conjure him into a holly tree that Walter himself had planted. 'You may stay there,' his spirit was told, 'and not emerge for as long as this holly grows green'. That was four centuries ago, and whether that tree or its descendant still flourishes, despite the quarrying away of the cave in the 1840s, I wouldn't know.

Even at the beginning of the nineteenth century something unpleasant was still active in Calverley Hall, pressing down on a visiting Wesleyan minister's chest as he slept in bed, and then tossing him out on to the floor not once, but three times, around the hour of midnight. Eighty years or so later, the church bells started to ring inexplicably at 1 a.m. one night and the villagers turned up only to find the church door locked. Even when the keys were located the mystery remained unsolved, for as soon as the key rattled in the lock, the ringing stopped. Nevertheless, the locals pointed the finger at Walter's shade, 'Owd Calverley', as they had when the minister had been tipped out of bed. Walter's taste for a life of incident did not, it seemed, end with his awful death. Perhaps the circumstances of his life even enhanced it.

The two murdered boys, William and Walter, found their rest inside Calverley Church. Their father was buried at York, supposedly. Some say he was moved back to Calverley and lies in an unmarked grave in the church, along with sixteen previous generations of Calverleys and his sons.

Local tragedies like this are rare, and local lads in Victoria's time found the whole story enticing and exciting. Enough, indeed, to gather in the churchyard, throw their caps in a pile and join hands in a ring around them. Then they would solemnly intone a rhyme that was said to call up the ghost of Old Walter Calverley. 'Old Calverley, Old Calverley, I'll have thee by the ear, I'll cut thee into collops unless thee appear', they chanted, stepping purposefully in a ring. Some of them would be delegated to go off and whistle through the keyholes in the church doors, repeating the chant. They reckoned that if they did it right the ghost would appear from the church – and once it apparently did. The boys fled, leaving their caps behind…

Now the family has gone from the hall and the clatter of the mills drove away the headless horse and drowned out the hoof-beats in Calverley Woods, before the mills themselves were silenced by the changes of the centuries. The hall was broken up into seven separate dwellings long ago and is now awaiting restoration as a holiday home of some distinction. I can't tell you the last time a Calverley lived there, although in a way Walter always will, through this tale. Or perhaps he is still waiting in the corridor for something to set off one of his bouts of bad behaviour.

Well, as I say, this isn't the only tale they tell of Walter Calverley's shocking life and its aftermath. While some say his act was driven by evil madness, others claim it was the pressure of debt and remorse for making a misery of the lives of at least two women, depriving his children of a reputable and prosperous future and perhaps of passing his dreadful temper on to them. Where the truth really lies I'm sure I don't know. But I do know that some events are so shocking and fearful that they soon go beyond their factual basis into a world of incomprehension that adds to both the notoriety and the legend-like retelling of the event.

Twelve

Mystery Visitors

The behaviour of the men in our legends frequently leaves much to be desired, and one might legitimately wonder why women were so often reviled as malevolent witches, while plenty of the men around them were violent boors or butchers, and sometimes both. However, it often happens in legendry, as in real life, that a woman will overcome man's evil and the world may be glad of it.

Shady Doings at Illingworth and Sheepridge

Churchgoing on Sunday used to be much more of a social obligation, and five centuries ago there weren't so many churches to choose from, even if you chose to choose. Each parish had its mother church and that was where you went. This even applied to cases like Halifax, the third largest parish in the country at 124sq miles, where the journey to church could be taxing to say the least. Imagine, for instance, if you lived in Heptonstall, the hilltop village about 10 miles away, where sometimes it seems the rain and wind are more familiar than the sun and soft breeze; or at the far reaches of Heptonstall township, on the moors! After a week of hard work, Sunday might not be your favourite day. If such remote households didn't make it to the mother church in Halifax, surely few churchmen could decry their commitment. It's no surprise that Heptonstall got the first chapel-of-ease in old Halifax Parish, making it a lot easier for remote parishioners.

But in the upper reaches of the Hebble Brook there was less excuse, though the obligation must still have been tiresome at times. Tiresome, and perhaps a little stressful, too, as leaving your home for several hours while the family went to church and back could have amounted to a robber's licence for some homes; and so often someone was left behind, perhaps one of the servants, to keep an eye on things.

One of the oldest houses in the Illingworth district is Fold Farm, once known as Mixenden Old Hall. It apparently has its priest's holes, for the hiding of Roman Catholic priests after the prohibition of their faith, and it has its ghosts; memories of the events that proved to be turning points for the inhabitants.

Two apparitions are reported: the first is a figure in an old rocking-chair and the second is a woman dressed in an apron, sitting at the foot of the stairs in the adjoining Cottage Fold. Are these really the two principal characters in what may be the Old Hall's most dreadful experience? Or are they two separate characters from two separate incidents, one now forgotten?

Fold Farm is a fine building sitting on the hillside overlooking what was once a beautiful and very rural valley. Back in the early sixteenth century it was the Old Hall and would have looked rather different, as would the whole landscape. We'd have to take away the concentration of buildings in the valley and the hillside behind, most of the roads and stone walls and of course modern intrusions like pylons to get even a hint of what it was like then. Nonetheless, there was a reasonably sizeable local population engaged in farming and textile work, and tracks leading across the moors to nearby towns. In other words, it wasn't entirely out of the way.

On Sundays the household attended church in Halifax and on one of these Sundays they left a maid to prepare the dinner and keep an eye on the house. She was pottering about the kitchen, cooking and taking advantage of having the house to herself, which released the pressure a bit, when a knock came at the door.

She answered it and at the door stood a fellow in travelling clothes, looking a bit wind-blown and weary.

'Sorry t' intrude, missus', he says. 'Ah've just walked ovver from Addin'ham, and it's a bit wild aht there and it's a long traipse too. Might ah trouble thee for a sup and a bite and a sit by t' fire f'r a speace?'

Well, the maid thought he looked a bit rough, but then surely anyone would who's hiked over the hills on a morning like that, and she remembered how the master had always stressed how travellers need a bit of kindness after they'd come over the hills, so she let him in.

'Sit thee dahn 'ere, lad, and warm thisen while I get you sommat', and she placed him in a rocking chair near the fire, a warm seat that brought the steam rising from his cloak in no time as he sat drinking the small beer and a heel of bread and cheese that she brought him.

He didn't seem to fancy talking much, so the maid assumed he was tired after his journey and got on with the cooking. Occasionally, she glanced over at the man, quietly sitting and obviously falling asleep by the fire.

'Aye, and I know nothing abaht 'im', she thought. 'I 'ope 'e's not a wrong 'un, as the master'll be away a bit yet. Still, 'e might be a quiet type, but 'e's done nowt wrong – not yet, anyhow', and she went on with the chores, glancing over at him from time to time.

Suddenly, the man gave a loud and deep snore, so loud that even the fellow himself seemed to jump in his chair, and so loud that the maid jumped! 'Well, I nivver,' she said, 'what a noise!' and she looked across at him where he sat with his head back, his mouth wide open, and snoring that hard, she thought, that he might rattle all the pans and dishes in the kitchen. As she watched, the man shifted again in his seat and his cloak, wrapped tightly across his legs, fell aside, revealing a pistol stuck in his belt.

The maid was dumbstruck – all her fears rose straight to mind at once. 'What kind o' man goes out on a Sunday wi' a pistol in 'is belt? 'E is a wrong'un!' she thought. 'There's a big pistol and ah'm sure he means no good wi' it, ah'll bet he's cum here to rob the ahse! Aye, an' woe to anybody 'ere when 'e wakes up, I'll be bound. That's me!', and she looked round in a rising panic. A host of thoughts were running about in her mind, none of them good. She needed to do something, to find something, anything to stop this ruffian from doing God knew what.

Well, the first thing she laid her eyes on wasn't the heavy iron fire tongs, nor any of the sharp knives that lay here and there around the kitchen, but the pan of meat with the hot fat sizzling and spitting away. She grabbed it and with no further thought tipped the fat into the man's open mouth and down his throat.

With his head stretched back as it was, it went straight down and he woke up, screaming in a frightful bubbly howl. He reached for his pistol, so she threw the pan itself at him and he dropped the weapon on the floor. He jumped up out of the chair at her, though how much he could see in his agony, who can imagine? He probably just knew there was a cause of this pain, and went for the shape of the likely cause. But she was already skitting away across the kitchen floor, screaming. She made for the stairs – away, away from this horrific scalded figure making such a dreadful rasping noise in his throat as he staggered towards her. The dogs were barking outside and her heart was in her mouth. To her relief the poor man never made it as far as the kitchen door – he collapsed with a terrible gurgling in his throat that seemed to echo right down through his heart and belly, vomiting some ghastly fluid till he finally lay silent and still. She sat down at the foot of the stairs and wept and shook, and waited.

Well, when the family came home there was a pan and the joint of meat on the floor, pools of hot fat staining the flags and scarring the old rocking chair, a pistol, and a man's body. All over there was the pungent smell of hot fat and burnt flesh. From behind the closed door to the stairs they heard a sobbing, and there they found the maid. Bit by bit they coaxed the full story out of her.

The terrible doings at the Old Hall were soon known throughout the neighbourhood and suddenly no one felt safe any more – they cried out that 'something should be done'. Some left off going to church rather than traipse religiously all the way down to town and back every Sunday, and that roused the powers-that-be to action. Not too long after, preparations were set in motion for a new chapel-of-ease at Illingworth, just a few hundred yards away from the Old Hall. By 1525 there was a new church on the hill: a local church, at last, for local people.

And the maid? Well, she swore she'd find somewhere else to work; she'd rather work in an inn than somewhere tempting to robbers. But the master declared she was better than a kennel full of dogs and, basking in the admiration of her household and neighbours, she was persuaded to stay on, ready to tell her story to whomsoever might ask when she had a bit of free time.

Whether the dead man had ever intended to rob the house, of course, was never discovered – but then it was too late for him anyway.

There I am, giving him the benefit of the doubt, and so I should, without proof, but very similar West Yorkshire stories, perhaps from around the same time, leave less room for doubt.

Take the woman who called in at Newhouse Hall in Sheepridge one day. Once again it was a Sunday and all the family were off at church in Huddersfield, with only a couple of the staff left to mind the house. Thinking no ill when a ragged and rough-looking woman begged for a drink and to sit by the fire, the maid let her in and continued to busy herself at her tasks. The woman was evidently tired and not inclined to much conversation, and soon dozed off by the fire. That suited the maid well enough; she had jobs to attend to before the family got home and if the visitor was asleep she wouldn't need watching.

Meanwhile, another servant was upstairs, cleaning the bedrooms, and as she glanced through the windows overlooking Lower Felgreave Woods she thought she saw something. She looked a bit more carefully – something was moving out there in the woods, but she couldn't quite make it out. 'Poachers?' she thought. She stepped back a pace or two, further into the shade of the room, and waited and watched. Yes, there was definitely movement in the woods and it did seem to be a group of figures moving around – not in the way they might move if they were just walking through the woods or collecting firewood, but altogether more furtively. Poachers then. It wouldn't be the first time, and she didn't begrudge the odd small beast for one of the village families. 'But then,' she thought, 'seems there's a few of 'em and poachers don't usually work in numbers'. She decided to go downstairs and have a word with the other girl.

As chance would have it, the other servant was on her way to see her and they met in the hall body. The kitchen girl was as troubled at the maid because she'd just noticed something strange about the visitor snoring away by the fire – she was wearing trousers beneath her skirts! That was no woman, she was sure, and those rough features had the look of a man, too! Now she heard that there were more men moving about in the woods behind the house, she began to get distressed. 'What shall we do?' she whispered, beginning to shake and tremble all over. 'They mean to rob us, for sure. We could be slain where we stand!'

The other servant was older and had a calmer – and crueller – head on her shoulders. 'Something smells good', she said. 'What have you got cooking in there?'

The maid, somewhat taken aback by the change of conversation, stammered a bit as she replied 'J-j-just the roast for the dinner.'

'Ah, and you're catching the fat?'

'Umm – yes.'

'Some people say fat's bad for you, you know, but that one by the fire looks as if she could do wi' some fattening up, and a good hot drink, if you get my meaning… I'll stay out here and be ready if there's any trouble.'

The younger girl's eyes widened, but she went back into the kitchen with this bit of advice. Oh, it was fearful advice, but the thought of what might happen if she didn't follow it was even more fearful. She picked up that pan of fat, and despite her trembling, managed to get a good portion of it down the visitor's throat. Of course, the same kind of scene ensued as we've heard about at Mixenden – the agony, the screaming, the terribly scalded visitor getting up and coming for the girl, reaching for something under his cloak. But just as the other maid came running in from the hall-body with a heavy poker, the master returned, and burst through the door to see what the noise was all about. It didn't take him long to size up the situation and draw his sword. In no time, the man's agony was ended and his blood pooled on the kitchen flags.

'Fetch some sand,' cried the master, breathing hard, 'and let's get this place cleaned up! It's Sunday, and we have better things to do than lay out thieves!' And that's how it was, for that intruder never got a Christian burial, nor any kind of burial come to that, for beneath Newhouse Hall there was an underground passage, and that's where the body was taken and tossed to rot in the darkness.

If the men skulking in the woods were no proof of wickedness afoot, and if the visitor's disguise was no final proof of evil intent, then one further thing was; as they were picking up the corpse from the kitchen floor, a whistle fell from his clothes. The family rejoiced that he'd never had time to blow the whistle, and never would.

Newhouse Hall must have rejoiced in astute servants, for another story tells a similar tale. In this, however, evil intent is more apparent, after a group of men arrived at the hall with a large crate one afternoon when the master was away. They told the servants that the master had sent it, with instructions that it be left in the upstairs corridor. So they took it upstairs, left it, and departed, and the staff got on with their work. But a maidservant in the corridor heard a noise within it, and went off to tell her colleagues. Suspicions aroused, they all resolved to keep watch until the master returned. One sat at one end of the corridor, and another at the other end. That night, around about midnight, with the whole house quiet, their suspicions were confirmed – the lid of the chest opened stealthily and a man began to climb out. That was the cue for the watchers to blow the whistles they had with them, and alert the other staff. The man fought back, perhaps unwisely, for in the unequal struggle that followed he was killed and his body, like that of the preceding tale, was tossed into that underground tunnel.

Now if archaeologists were to locate that tunnel, what would they make of what they find – assuming, of course, they find anything?

Thirteen

THE SPOILS
OF ILL-WILL

Sadly, the repertoire of folk narrative is full of the evil that men do, for tragedy thrives both on greed and on people's thirst for story. I'm reminded of a rhyme in an old ballad:

when men live in worldly wealth,
full few can have that grace
long in the same to keep themselves
contented with their place

To me, these lines always seem to be a commentary on life today as much as when they were written in the fourteenth century. However, we know our contemporary avarice all too well, but perhaps not the events of 650 years ago.

THE ELLAND FEUD

Elland today is a small post-industrial town on the banks of the River Calder, but if it seems a place of little account today, that certainly can't be said of it in the Middle Ages. Then, it was a bustling market town sited on a key crossing of the River Calder. Some say that had it not been for those miraculous head tales at Halifax, Elland might have become the major town of modern-day Calderdale. Be that as it may, Elland's fortunes fell nonetheless, perhaps its fortunes linked to the family who bore its name in the latter half of the 1300s.

Edward III was king when Sir John de Eland was Sheriff of Yorkshire and High Steward to the Earl of Warenne. Sir John was a powerful man, full of his own self-importance and evidently an ugly man with whom to quarrel. If West Yorkshire needs an exemplar of power misused, surely he would appear as a prime candidate; if it should need a story advising restraint over retaliation, then the story of the Elland Feud would be top of the list.

Sir John's family had only acquired their estate, it is said, by morally dubious means. At the time of Edward the Confessor, a young Norman by the name of Hugo Beaulieu visited Yorkshire in company with one of Earl Godwin's sons, and they were caught in one of our well-known storms. They took refuge at the home of Wilfrid, where Hugo met and was beguiled by Wilfrid's beautiful young wife, and he stayed rather longer than was appropriate. Before long, Wilfrid realised that something was going on, and challenged his guest to combat for the hand of the compromised woman. They fought in the hall, as the young wife looked on, and some say she even had a hand in the duel, rendering assistance to her young French lover. Wilfrid fell, mortally wounded, with a dagger in his chest. The lord's last act was to dip his hand into his own heart's blood, and cast it upon Beaulieu, 'Even as you gain this house, in the same manner shall you and all your kin quit it'. They also say that every descendant of Hugo and the faithless wife bore three red spots on their forehead.

Nonetheless, Hugo had his woman and his estate, and when William the Conqueror came to England he fought loyally for the new king from his homeland, and was rewarded. He was not long to enjoy the spoils, though. In 1069 when the dispossessed English rose, he fell by the hand of one of those evicted. In his dying breath, did he wonder if this was irony or the outcome of Wilfrid's curse?

But if it was the result of the curse it was imperfectly realised, for Hugo's kin held on to the estate for some while longer yet, and a man who declared that he feared 'neither man, nor God, nor Devil' became favoured by the king. Sir John de Eland had those three red spots and a passionate history; by the time he enters this story he had already married three times. He was confident of his own power, whether by sword, by law, or in royal favour, so his pride was allowed full rein and his anger had no natural check.

So it was unwise of young Exley to kill a nephew of Sir John's – though it may have been part of a major disagreement between the Warenne and Lacy families over another defecting wife. Alice de Lacy had taken up with one of the Warennes and perhaps such a deadly skirmish was unsurprising, especially as the killing occurred while the 'injured party', the Lacys, were laying siege to the Warennes' Conisborough Castle.

Still, compensation for the nephew's death was required, and Exley knew it. In acknowledgment of his culpability he made Eland a gift of land. The land was accepted, of course, but as far as Eland was concerned, it was not enough – only Exley's life itself could atone for the loss of his nephew. Exley thought it wise to put some barrier between himself and Eland's murderous wrath, and took refuge with Sir Robert Beaumont of Crosland Hall.

Eland and Beaumont did not get on at all, and when Sir John heard that Beaumont had given Exley shelter, he took it as a direct affront, and an excuse to act upon a long-held grudge over land that Sir John had coveted. He wanted Exley and he was prepared to take him by force.

Yet Beaumont was strong, too, and he had good allies that would assist him in any showdown. Hugh of Quarmby and Lockwood, of Lockwood Hall, were kin of his and lived nearby. Their support was taken for granted when Beaumont argued that Exley had made due recompense and was now entitled to respite. Eland snarled in his den, and concocted a scheme that he thought would surely quieten dissent in his neighbourhood.

One day in May, Eland decided it was time to act. He called a group of armed men together, and as night fell they set off – but not for Crosland Hall. Instead, they headed for Quarmby Hall, to the west of Huddersfield, and took it by surprise. Before long, Hugh of Quarmby was dead and the raiders were again on the trail. This time they headed south-east to Lockwood, and again they left the property with blood on their hands and in the hall. With Beaumont's key allies dead, it was time to proceed to Crosland Hall, a few miles away to the south-west.

Crosland Hall had one key advantage – a moat. When the raiders arrived they were obliged to stay their passions, and wait – but not for long, because the house stirred and those who stirred first, as always, were the servants, and a maid was sent for the morning's milk. She lowered the drawbridge, and that was all the raiders needed. In they rushed, and into the hall, meeting stiff resistance from the servants and retainers, but they got through them all to Beaumont's bedchamber and dragged him from his bed. His wife shrieked as she, too, was dragged out. Despite all the house's struggles, the raiders were victorious. In due course a number of bodies, including Exley's, were laid out around the house, and the survivors were gathered in the Great Hall. The couple and their two sons stood captives of Sir John and his men, awaiting his decision. Death was expected, surely, but not in the form the witnessed by his wife and children – for there in the hall the head of Robert Beaumont, Lord of Crosland Hall, was severed from his body.

But Eland was not yet done. Surely already drunk from the night's bloody endeavours, he decided that it was time for his band to celebrate with their hosts. The servants were commanded to bring wine, ale, meat and bread, and the family to sit with Sir John. Beaumont's widow was commanded to act the host's part, and to hand him his tankard for him to toast her in her hour of loss. Then the two children were invited to share the gloomy repast; but the elder, Adam, then about five years old, was having none of it, and threw the bread back at his father's murderer. Eland was angry, but impressed, 'See this child,' he declared, 'see how well he can take his father's death! I warrant if there be any that will avenge this night, it will be he'. Then, mindful of his own power, he leant forward, 'But mind, boy, and all here, if he or any shows any inclination to revenge, then each of those threats shall be cut off, one by one, just as we have tonight – we will weed them out from our midst, just as we weed the corn'. Yet for the moment, in a show of some clemency, the mother and her boys were spared, as were the offspring of Quarmby and Lockwood.

Meanwhile, across the high hills between Lancashire and Yorkshire were headed other allies of Beaumont, alerted by messenger when the attack had begun. They were met on the way with the news that they were already too late to help the lords, and turned back. The Towneleys and Breretons soon took the mothers and children of the afflicted families into Lancashire for safety, while Sir John relaxed in the afterglow of his brutal behaviour. People talked in shock of his deed, for sure, but none knowing of his propensity for direct action would complain, nor set the matter to law. And so Sir John of Eland remained secure in his post for another fifteen years.

The sons of the slain lords grew up as young men should in those days, skilled with weapons and proud of their heritage, not a little angry and not a little rash. Several men evidently had cause to regret coming into their company at fairs and other gatherings, and nursed their memory with bruises and lighter pockets. So it would seem they were perhaps well-skilled in the casual violence of teenagers in all periods when Lockwood spoke up one day. 'My friends, do you not think it may be time for us to avenge our fathers?'

The others stopped, and looked at each other. Adam Beaumont mused aloud. 'That was a cruel deed, hateful to all humanity, and he threatened to weed me out like a weed in corn should I try to avenge him. Let him try!'

'We have each seen our fathers slain by the foul Eland,' continued Lockwood, 'and as for me I can hardly keep my patience with each passing year. For too long has he taken his pleasure of his lands while we skulk, our rightful homes tended by retainers. It is time, surely, to go home, friends, and remove the one obstacle to us enjoying our inheritance!'

So the young men conferred and planned and communicated with friends in their home country, and they learnt the doings of Sir John. Two men, Dawson and Haigh, bore them important information – Eland made it a point to always attend the tournament at Brighouse and returned via Cromwell Bottom. The wood there, they thought, would make an excellent spot for an ambush…

And so it came about that the three young men lay in wait at Brookfoot, with a number of armed followers, and from a hilltop looked over the road from Brighouse. At length, Sir John, as they had been told, appeared with his retinue. Fearing naught and not recognising the young men when he encountered them on the road, he doffed his cap in customary courtesy.

'Oh, knight', spoke Adam, 'do not think that your courtesy counts for anything with me, or indeed with any of us.'

'Really? So are you thieves or murderers, haunting this lonely lane like foul boggarts?'

'We are avengers, Sir John, weeds that have grown strong under careful nurture. Adam Beaumont, at your service, Sir Knight, and with me the heirs of Quarmby and Lockwood'. Adam bowed in his saddle.

'Then my greetings to you all, young sirs, and better I had weeded you as I promised – but be warned that any harm you do me will be reckoned by others, and I would counsel you to retreat.'

'We'll have our own reckoning first, for sure', cried William Lockwood, starting forward, and Eland threw himself, sword swinging, at Adam Beaumont, while their respective bands fought on the road behind. Eland fought against the young men as well as his reputation affirmed, but outnumbered and with no benefit of age, he finally found his sword cast from his hands. And finally, the heirs of Quarmby, Lockwood and Beaumont had their revenge, and Sir John de Eland lay in blood on the road.

The attackers rode off back west across the hills and took refuge in Furness, in the Lake District. One deed was done but they were still not free to return to their homes; for if they had sought and found their revenge, might not the son of Sir John, now heir to the estate, also seek such revenge? No matter that the new lord's reputation was one of benevolence, how could he overlook the death of his father, even if he acknowledged the original cause? Such was Adam's reasoning as they wintered in the fells, and so the stage was set for another episode in their revenge. When they heard that the new Sir John was petitioning the king for redress of his father's murder, there seemed just cause for further action. As the old Sir John had threatened to do to them, but never carried out, so they would do to his family. But this time the threat would not be spoken, but simply carried out.

On the eve of Palm Sunday the next year, the young men were gathered again in Yorkshire. Once again they had information on their quarry's activities and they broke into Elland Mill to await the young lord's passage to church the next day. Their tense rest was interrupted too early, however. Sunday notwithstanding, the miller had need of corn and sent his wife to fetch some from the mill. She blundered into the young men, who bound her and laid her aside, lest she should raise the alarm. Back at home her husband raged at his wife's delay and resolved to beat the idleness out of her. So off he went himself to the mill; for his pains and intent he ended up trussed beside her.

That night in Elland Hall, the young knight was sleeping fit-fully, plagued by a dream that he was being attacked, and defeated. He told his wife of his dream, but she didn't take dreams seriously and made light of it. 'Husband,' she said, 'one thing I know – this morning we are going to church, and no outrageous dream will turn us aside'. John bowed his assent to her rational words, but he made sure he put some armour beneath his clothing and took some stoutly armed men with them.

Thus the party approached the mill en route to the church, and thus the dream spoke true – Beaumont stepped out and shot an arrow straight at Sir John, which glanced off his hidden breastplate. Tumult broke out as Lockwood stepped up, crying, 'Cousin, you shoot wide!' and loosed his own arrow, which again did no harm to their intended victim. Eland challenged them as the affray started in earnest, 'If this town knew of this – and believe me they will – then you would surely never dare to show your face here! You can only do your work in this cowardly manner!' He was confident of his town's support, and even as he spoke the hue and cry was being raised, horns being sounded and the bells of Elland Church being rung backwards, a recognised alarum signal. Lockwood knew time was short and this time he aimed at Sir John's head. He did not miss, and in the melée Sir John's son was injured too. While the assailants took off down White Hill Lane towards Old Earth, the boy was taken to Elland Hall, where he died. And with the boy went the line that was set up by Hugo Beaulieu's deceit three centuries before, and the estate passed from the Elands to the family of the young John's wife, the Saviles.

Meanwhile, Beaumont and his companions were fleeing Elland's jurisdiction, but their progress was slower than they would have liked. Quarmby had been injured in the attack and Lockwood was helping him along. When they got to Ainley Wood, however, Quarmby prevailed on them. As the people of Elland were already on their trail, it would do no good if they were all caught because of his injury. He pressed his wallet on Lockwood as they hid him in the midst of an old ivy tree; away, they hoped, from the eyes of their pursuers. 'Take this,' he said, 'and in your mirth remember me – rather that, than our enemies enjoy it if they find me'. They clasped hands, and parted.

And so Beaumont and Lockwood made off through the wood and escaped into Huddersfield, as the Elland folk unknowingly passed by Quarmby in their haste. The pursuers, carrying their bows, staves and rusty bills came to the extent of Eland authority and turned back. As they retraced their steps through the wood, one of their number, aware of the ways of birds, was drawn by the chattering of crows and magpies to an old ivy tree and there they found Quarmby, bleeding. The frustrated posse finished him there and then and dragged his body back to town as their only prize.

Lockwood and Beaumont escaped that day, and Adam took up his old family residence in Crosland Hall, though taking care not to venture into Eland's jurisdiction, where the Under-Sheriff, Bosville, was determined to apprehend his master's killers.

William Lockwood, however, fell prey to a young man's most ready undoing; he fell in love with a woman too close to danger.

They used to meet in Emley Park, at an old oak tree hollowed out with age. It was a suitable hiding place for lovers, but not as secret as they might have wished, for Bosville heard of their relationship and turned it to his advantage. Some say he had a word with the young lady and suggested she reveal their next meeting – or he would see her and her family turned out of their home. Others will have it that Bosville had an informant who had spotted them several times in the old tree, and he staked it out. However it happened, Lockwood was a marked man, and it seems everybody knew and took it seriously, but himself.

One day, hurrying to meet the girl, he ran into two young ladies, cousins of his. 'Cousin,' they implored, 'we know of your love for the girl at Emley and can suppose your errand now – but take our advice and do not go, not today, for Bosville is waiting and she will prove false to you. Come with us now, cousin – we are headed for Crosland and you can make safety there'. Lockwood tried to make light of their warning, but they were adamant. Yet still he could not pass up his tryst so easily. He was sure his love was true and that he could not leave her waiting in vain. 'Cousins, I thank you, and will join you at Crosland shortly, after our farewells have been said', he replied and he rode on.

Glad was Lockwood's heart when he reached the old oak tree safely and greeted his love warmly; but sorry was he soon after, when Bosville's men encircled the tree. A hollow tree allows reasonable protection, however, and the couple shrank back into the trunk, Lockwood firing his bow and keeping the assailants at bay – but he must have known that it was only a matter of time. He could not have reckoned on when or how it would end. For Bosville threatened to set fire to the girl's house if he did not give up, and offered terms that sounded as favourable as a hunted but aristocratic fugitive might hope for. Lockwood was not convinced, but the girl threw her arms around him and as she did so she cut the string of his bow. Her lover was stunned, and pushed her out of the tree.

'Fie on you, woman, and all your kind – you were ever destined to be men's downfall', and he shouted out to the men encircling them as he shrank back into the tree, 'Let you all take this woman as an example, and look to yourselves.'

Bosville settled into negotiation mode, praising him for a brave man and assuring him of his understanding over the revenge murders, offering Lockwood the good terms he had promised before. Lockwood knew he didn't have any hope except to trust him. He stepped out of the tree and handed over his sword, dagger and useless bow, and consented to be bound in accordance with the law. And then, in front of his treacherous lover, helplessly bound, he was slain outright beside the tree which had once given him such hope. And that tree became known as the Lady Oak, they say, after the treacherous girlfriend, and its roots were only grubbed up in 1939. Nearby stood a stone erected by the locals in memory of Lockwood's betrayal.

Two of the vengeful sons had now fallen; just Adam Beaumont remained alive. What the cousins had tried to persuade Lockwood was that Bosville was pursuing writs against the two of them from the court in London, overriding local jurisdiction. Adam Beaumont at least took heed of the warning and took himself overseas to France. There he secured a good position as a Crusader in the Knights of Rhodes, and acquitted himself bravely, we are assured, in many battles until finally he fell in Hungary fighting against the Turks.

Back at home the Eland and Lockwood families were no more, and the cycle of revenge passed into the care of the scribes who kept the history of their times and the more romantic tongues of storytellers and balladeers.

Fourteen

SMILING MEN WITH BAD REPUTATIONS

Folklore can ruin a person's reputation. It can, for instance, recall the messier details of a life that the more obsequious biographer might choose to gloss over. Was Walter Calverley a passionate but repentant scion of an old and respectable family, driven to a lethal breakdown by financial crisis? Or was he an abusive, manipulative and profligate drunk, naturally given to acts of rage and violence? Popular tales prefer a spicier account to explain their ghosts.

Yet popular account can also blacken a reputation without seeming cause, at least not to the modern reader. Many an old woman, maliciously accused by her neighbours of witchcraft, might have vouched for this. When Old Betty i' th' Stones, who lived near Todmorden, was seen larking about going head over heels in a field, more like a hare than a mature lady, it was enough to set off the rumour that she was a witch rather than – as we might think – simply a lady of high and eccentric spirits. Whatever the cause, the likelihood is that people would stop talking so freely and maybe that's at the root of the problem. It's easier to believe things of people who are in some way marginalised, either by themselves or by their neighbours.

Rimington's Ride

Perhaps James Rimington should have talked to people more; he might have learned what people thought of him. His legend certainly puzzled his biographers, and thus ourselves today. They all seem to have thought Rimington, who was steward for the Kaye family, was not only good at his job but also admirably fair with regards both to the Kayes who employed him and the tenants who would have had good cause to fear an unsympathetic steward. Nonetheless, there was apparently some element of popular rejoicing when he died on 16 December 1696, so you'd think there might well be something we haven't been told. But there's no point guessing. The rejoicing ended soon enough when people realised that Rimington hadn't really gone away at all.

It seems to have started with strange noises being heard from Rimington's Closet, as his room at the hall was known. What noises we don't know, but then any noises from a room recently vacated by the death of its occupant would be disquieting. If it had just been noises in the room, people would probably just have got used to it and it would have become just another haunting in an old hall.

But old Rimington rode out, and was reported to be seen at times riding pell-mell down Woodsome Lane holding two equally frenzied hounds on a leash. So fast did they go that as they passed through Farnley village, they once plucked a large nail from a house doorpost! That was enough to convince the locals of the reality of their ghost – surely real enough to do them harm if they got in the way – and they called on the local clergy to help them.

Well, there are lots of things the clergy can do, but they don't always work. Sometimes they're obliged to bring out the big guns and ritually 'lay' an unquiet spirit, and that's what they did to this one. They coaxed him into his old room and there charged him to remain quiet as long as the holly trees grow green (a traditional exhortation that we have of course met before). Some said that he had actually been changed into a robin that could still be seen returning to his old room. This belief that a robin is a ghost is why, they say outside the village, Farnley people get called Farnley Robinets.

Black Dick

Over 100 years earlier, Sir Richard Beaumont of Whitley Hall, near Mirfield, also acquired a reputation that historians are somewhat unsure about. He lived in a time (1574-1631) when powerful men needed to be duplicitous for their own sakes. But the double life of 'Black Dick', as he was known, might make for an investigation as dramatic as that of Jack the Ripper. Beaumont was a lord and was buried as one, with his own tomb in the church of St John the Baptist, Kirkheaton. But popular report had it that he was also a gambler (like many of his class), a philanderer (likewise), a profligate (again, not especially unique among gentlemen of the upper classes) and a callous highwayman. Now that's where Dick's character turns rather darker, and the main story about him positively paints him black.

A stagecoach was robbed on the Wakefield Road and a passenger killed. Who did it? Well, among the popular suspects was Richard Beaumont, the nobleman with an alleged shadowy side, but nothing could be more than rumour. Yet one person suspected this and was sure enough of his conclusions to confront him. The accuser was an acquaintance, possibly a highwayman himself, familiar with the methods of others, and he hit upon what he thought would be a rather safer, and even kinder, way to come about a large sum of money than holding up coaches.

There was a tunnel – maybe there still is – running from Whitley Hall to the summer house in the grounds, and that was where the man met with Black Dick and laid out his very good reasons for associating him with the Wakefield Road robbery, as well as the very good sense involved in Beaumont parting with a certain amount of cash. Inevitably, the threat of blackmail led to a fight and the two drew their swords and went at it in the tunnel. Beaumont's assailant was the stronger, and the nobleman was pushed down and finally killed and decapitated by his would-be blackmailer.

Did that end the highway robbery in the locality? Unlikely, but it started another ghost legend, in which Black Dick walks at ground level between the hall and the summer house, with his own head tucked beneath his arm, at midnight on 5 July every year. And somewhere along the line he picked up other tales; that his bloody hand was hidden behind a mantelpiece in the house, whilst the ghost of one of the several ladies he beguiled in the hall was reported in the 1880s, gliding in white about the house.

Whitley Hall has now vanished, demolished in the middle of the last century, and alas no skeletal hand was found, and spare a thought for a homeless ghost. But one witness to this story remains: Black Dick's Tower. This is the hilltop remains of the summer house, except that the building we see postdates the story... Also, and sadly for the story, Black Dick was actually given his nickname by King James I when he knighted him, and died naturally at home on 20 October 1631. But if you ask which version people would prefer to believe, look no further than another local tradition. Until Kirkheaton Church was rebuilt after a fire in 1886, his statue was reputed to sit up whenever the clock struck midnight. I suppose there's no reason, though, why he shouldn't have been a highwayman as well as a baronet and MP for Pontefract.

So some rumours, like Betty's, are born of nonsense; others may arise from a sense of grievance or resentment for those in positions of power. Beaumont and Rimington perhaps fell victim to the latter, for surely at some point somebody would have felt hard done by at their hands and told their friends and neighbours exactly why they felt so. The written words of the chroniclers stay with us; the spoken resentments are lost to time. Yet even with this undeniable bias in recorded history, the dissociation between reputation and chronicle can be surprising.

THE SUICIDAL SCULPTOR

Coming closer to our time, a huge crowd assembled at Ward's End in Horton Street, Halifax, in September 1864 to witness the unveiling of a new statue. Prince Albert had died almost three years before and it had been decided to raise a public fund for

Halifax's own commemorative monument. A leading sculptor – Thomas Thornycroft – was commissioned. Thornycroft had already embarked on perhaps his best-known work, the stirring statue of Boadicea on London's Victoria Embankment (never mind her intention to destroy the city of London utterly when she set off on her revolutionary path). So on the unveiling day in Halifax, lots of local VIPs marched up from their fine new Town Hall in a grand procession watched by around 10,000 people. When they got to the statue, the bands played and the covering was pulled off an imposing bronze sculpture of Prince Albert sitting on a handsome horse. Children were lifted high and the people cheered, but some thought, 'Eh? Summat's wrong 'ere'. And neighbour spoke to neighbour, and it was, 'Horses don't walk like that, d' they?'

'Not tharrI've seen.'

'That sculptor's got yon nag's legs wrong, sithee.'

'Aye, 'appen 'e 'as, an' all. Eh, if it tried t' walk like that, it'd fall ovver!'

'What're they gonna do abaht that, then, eh?'

And so it went on, and the rumour spread through town that the legs were wrong. More than that, some started to say that Thornycroft had realised his mistake after seeing it up there on the pedestal, and was so mortified that he committed suicide! People will still tell you that today, even after the statue was moved from Ward's End in 1900, because of traffic congestion (they had it in those days too) to Albert Park beside Skircoat Road, where it stands now.

Well it's a good story, so why not tell it? After all, it's told of other sculptors in other places – like the statue of King William in Hull, where the sculptor, Peter Scheemakers, was shamed into topping himself, they said, by forgetting to put in a saddle, or stirrups, or spurs…

Thomas Thornycroft, seems to have come in for a bit of stick at the hands of the populace and apparently achieved the feat of killing himself at least twice. He was also commissioned to do an equestrian Albert at Wolverhampton, and he posed the horse in the same way. The folk in Wolverhampton, just as in Halifax, said, 'if a horse walked like that, it'd fall over', and they drew the same fatal conclusion from their judgment.

So much for the reputation of Thomas Thornycroft. Now let's set the record straight for the poor fellow. Our Thomas died a natural death in 1885, at seventy years of age, twenty years or more after his statues at Halifax and Wolverhampton were unveiled. As for the horse – well, its name was Nimrod and it was the prince's favourite mount; it's pictured in a stance called ambling. That's a way of riding that has to be trained into a horse, and involves moving both limbs of each side alternately. This might sound awkward – and looked wrong to the spectators, as we know – but produces a comfortable movement for the rider. Doubtless this was Prince Albert's favourite way of riding.

As for the Scheemakers' statue in Hull, it's true; King Billy doesn't have any of those things, but then he's supposed to be riding in the classical style of Roman emperors. Oh, and Scheemakers died forty-seven years after the unveiling in 1734.

When it comes down to it, I suppose most of us prefer the company of the storyteller to the pedant.

Fifteen

TALK OF THE DEVIL

When we hear of brutal acts like those of Walter Calverley and John de Eland, it isn't altogether surprising that people believe in the Devil. Some behaviour goes so far beyond humanity that it's easier and perhaps more reassuring to believe it is inspired by some implacable agency of evil, a presence always at our side.

THE DEVIL'S KNELL

Maybe that was what was in Thomas of Soothill's mind when he contemplated his latest fit of rage back in the fifteenth century. He had been angry at one of his servants – not too unusual in itself, he reflected – but then he went and killed the poor man and threw his corpse into Forge Dam, a nearby mill-pond. That was unusual, and when he had calmed down he felt rather bad about it, as indeed he should. So he made penance for his crime and thinking how the Devil had surely got into him, he did something which he hoped would help to ward the Old Lad off from his part of West Yorkshire at least; he contributed a tenor bell to his local church at Dewsbury.

Thus it is that every Christmas Eve, after some careful calculations, the Devil's Knell is tolled at Dewsbury Minster – one toll for each year since Christ's birth and the final toll sounding at the very point of midnight. Not that the Church will claim that the knell chases away the Devil, as that's far too superstitious for them; they'd far rather say that it simply celebrates Christ's victory over the old adversary. But local people might have seen it differently, superstitious or not. And it's nice to think that if it works as intended by Thomas nearly 600 years ago, we in West Yorkshire should have to tolerate fewer devilries for another year.

We do have a very adversarial culture at times, yet Lucifer was not created to be the enemy of God – far from it. There was a time when the two got on perfectly well, until the little misunderstanding that resulted in the War in Heaven. After that things got pretty tetchy between God and the Devil. The Devil always claimed it was humans that came between him and the deity he thought was his best mate, so he's been taking it out on us ever since and getting us to take sides and come over to his place when we've had enough of things here.

Well, it's our own fault. We give him just enough attention to keep him interested, I reckon, and he's kept popping up over the centuries. One of his most spectacular appearances in West Yorkshire was in Shelley, around 1760. Sometimes the comeuppance for one's misdeeds can be rather more spectacular than even Eland and Calverley met.

So spare a thought, or perhaps a satisfied chuckle for the more vengeful among you, for a lawyer called Wright. Few people have a good word for lawyers, sadly, and it's probably because of people like Wright. He built himself a sound reputation in the district amongst those who could afford to pay for his services, though it seems to have been largely at the expense of widows, paupers and orphans. He managed to build himself a good fortune, too. People shook their heads and wondered how a man in his position could act so iniquitously. Anyway, that was how he chose to live his life, and if you were socially vulnerable you probably prayed you never had occasion to meet him.

Then one day he disappeared and was never seen again. His room at his home at Roydhouse was locked up securely when he disappeared, as without a body there was no evidence of his permanent absence. No one knew if he would return to take up his nefarious practice – and if he couldn't get into his office, he'd surely have you in court. The big question, of course, was where had he gone? His friends didn't know. Some of the local residents knew, however, and were ready to tell anybody who would listen.

'Tha' might've guessed from his wicked life, sithee', they said. 'That man 'ad sold his soul to the Auld Lad, and his every act was t' the Devil's honour. But any lawyer knows, if you make a deal with the Devil, you've to sign on t' line, wi' your name or an X'll do, and that reckoning i'n't easy to avoid. He's a better lawyer than 'em all. Wright must have known that his time was coming near, you know, but aye, he didn't go quietly!

'One night we heard a din and looked out o' t' windows, and what a flaysome sight did we see! There were this coach coming up the road, hell for leather it were going, and the two horses afore it running so fast it seemed like they were leaping 12yds with every stride. Maybe they were, because there were a funny light about that coach and as it got nearer we could see what it were – flames were comin' out o' them 'orses' nostrils! What a sight! We wanted to jump back in us beds, but we couldn't look away.

'And d' ye know, it stopped in our village, and it'll not surprise thee t' know it stopped outside that lawyer's place. And this big chap got out, smartly dressed an' all, but summat about 'im just as flaysome as them horses, and he went into the house. And then there were a kerfuffle – there were shoutin' and screamin' and kickin' and slammin' o' doors, and then this big chap comes out, and he's got the lawyer in 'is arms, wrapped tight. And Wright, 'e were strugglin' and makin' a racket, right up until 'e were slammed into t' back o' that coach, and then they were off agen, flamey breath an' all, racin' out o' t' village – an' that were the last we saw o' lawyer Wright.

'None of us got much sleep that night, I can tell you, and we didn't much like goin' near that house where the Auld Lad had been so familiar. But the landlord, he let it off, but the lawyer's room, where 'e did 'is work and mebbe that's where 'e did the deal wit' Fiend, that were locked up and no one wanted to go in there!

They were afraid they mightn't come out again, y' see, or if they did come out they mighta been touched by evil. There's supposed to be an old kist in that room, and who knows what's in it, and no one yet fancies finding out. Leave well alone, we all reckoned, and that's the way it's been since that night. Good riddance!'

That room stayed locked up for a long time, too. Just before the First World War, a writer told how two young men had finally volunteered to go in about thirty years previously. They found dust 3in deep – not surprising in a room that hadn't seen a broom for over a century! And there was indeed a chest on the floor, although no evil escaped when they opened it. They found, as you might expect in a lawyer's office, just a load of papers. Whether any of them testified to a solemn pact with the Devil, we'll never know, as soon afterwards folk were sent in to clean the room and the papers, unfortunately, went the way of the dust. Otherwise we might know how Wright got his reputation.

The Devil had his daft side, too. Apparently he rather liked some of the houses we live in, so he collected them. Maybe he had some kind of vernacular architecture museum in Hell, but one day he'd picked up a number of cottages from the Bradford area and was carrying them off in his apron. Alas, his brat-string (a brat being an apron, rather than a naughty child) broke with all the attractive little houses he'd picked up, and they fell out upon the hillside. Well, there was no doing anything about it there and then, so he left them there and thought he'd come back for them later when

he'd mended his apron, but it must have slipped his attention. The people who owned those houses found them there and decided it'd be a lot easier to accept their new location than move the house back where it had been. So that's how the village of Low Road came to be.

THE DEVIL'S ROCK

We can see that the Old Fellow has been quite familiar with West Yorkshire in the past. Wherever you see a 'Devil' place-name, 'Tuel' or 'Dule' here in West Yorkshire, that's where local folk think he's turned up or done something. Dhoul's Pavement, for instance, is what some people used to call the paved road into West Yorkshire across Blackstone Edge, implying who they thought was the most likely contractor on that particular job.

However, the Devil's never been too hard for a canny lad or lass to outwit. He's built bridges for us in return for the first soul to pass over it, forgetting to stipulate that it was a human soul he wanted; so say thank you to that poor dog when you cross the Devil's Bridge in Kirkby Lonsdale. He's also fired crossbow bolts at Aldborough from Howe Hill, and missed. Take a look at the giant megaliths, the Devil's Arrows, and think what a big fellow he was – and probably still is when the fancy takes him. Even the biggest fellows can fall short, as the story of Devil's Rock in Blackshaw Head demonstrates. Most people call it Great Rock, but if we call it that we might lose the story, so Devil's Rock it is. If you go there today you can see marks made by the Devil's foot long ago, from a time when he and God were still on relatively cordial terms – though it must be said, they were still rather competitive.

Tales from all sorts of places relate how these two rivals once got on well enough to take walks together. Apart from the chance of some feisty conversation, no doubt, they enjoyed looking over the lands of the earth and seeing how the humans were getting on, now that they were getting more used to the idea of free will. For sure, both of them saw an opportunity in all this.

So one day they were strolling along the range of hills we now call the Pennines, and they came to a headland overlooking a valley and some fine views towards Todmorden and Hebden Bridge. There's a big monument, an obelisk, on that headland today, called Stoodley Pike. Before that there was another monument and before that there was a cairn, so it's not the kind of place that gets forgotten or missed very easily. These two came up to it and looked out over the valley; there they spotted a couple of little towns and a scattering of farms and people going to and fro, and they decided to watch for a while and see what was going on.

It was a pleasant scene of industriousness, thought God. There they were getting on with the jobs they needed to do, growing a few crops and keeping a number of beasts, building sturdy houses and developing a nice little sideline in making cloth. A bit of resourcefulness and inventiveness among humans always justified his decisions, he thought, and he nodded smugly at his companion.

Now the Devil didn't disagree that God had done a good job of humanity and free will and all that (though he did wonder if it was really all his own work), but he thought God could sometimes see things a bit more rosily than they actually were. He knew from his own observations that humans could be a bad bit of work without any help from him, and that sometimes all he needed to do was offer a bit of advice rather than anything stronger. So when he looked out he saw something a bit different. He saw the folk having naked races in the main street, he saw fathers and husbands killing men whom they thought too close to their daughters or wives, men and women who turned neighbour against neighbour with just a few well-chosen words and men who shut larks up in boxes and took them along to sing in pubs. When he saw the chap catching rats in his teeth for a flagon of beer per rat and all the people watching him transfixed, he turned to God and said, 'You look pretty pleased with yourself, but I reckon this lot are bound for my place'.

This was nothing new, of course. They'd had this argument plenty of times before and it was nothing too serious. The Devil

made a claim on the souls of some community they came across and pointed out in his defence some of the dubious things the people were doing. God would argue that whatever they did, it wasn't the end of the matter. And in the end God would propose a wager and set his companion a task, and one of them would win the wager – usually God, it must be said, as he was pretty shrewd in setting the tasks. So they hardly bothered with the argument any more, they just got on with the wager. So God sighed and said, 'OK, there's one way we can settle this'.

'And what, Kind Deity, do you propose?'

'You see that great rock over there?'

The Devil squinted out across the valley. 'You mean that big lump sticking out of the hillside like a kneecap?'

'That's the one. Well, if you can step out from here and get over to that rock in one stride, then I'll not argue with you, you can have 'em, all these poor souls in this valley.'

'Well, let's see, it's about a mile over there… I'm a big, strong chap. I reckon I can do it, you're on!'

'About a mile and a half, I reckon', thought God, but he didn't say anything. He just smiled sweetly and indicated that his companion should go ahead and try.

So the Devil took a deep breath and took aim with his eye. He drew back his shoulders, stood to his full height and stepped off the crag – left foot first, of course.

Well, he stretched his leg as far as it would go and then he managed to push it just a little farther. As his foot landed heavily on the rock he grunted in satisfaction. All he had to do now was get his right leg over. He took another deep breath, steadied himself and then thought, 'Ah – this might not be as easy as I thought'. With growing unease, he prepared to step off with his right foot…

Of course, as soon as he did his left leg slipped off, right down the great rock's face and down the hillside. His right leg buckled underneath him as he tumbled, cursing, in a heap at the bottom of the valley. Oh, he did hate to hear God laughing up there above him, it brought back some unpleasant memories. But there it was, he'd lost his wager and he had to leave the folk in the valley to their own devices from then on. So he picked himself up, wiped off the mud and smiled ruefully. And the big fellows walked on.

Now I know you don't believe a word of it, but if you go that way now you'll see the hole on top of Devil's Rock that he left when his foot landed on its long stride from Stoodley Pike, which you'll see, too, far across the valley. And you'll see the great crack and rift in the rock that he left from top to bottom as his foot slipped, and if you follow the line of that crack you'll see how that damned foot just kept on sliding down the hill, leaving a gouge near-straight which the locals found useful for a track. So the proof is there in the landscape – if you know what to look for.

The Lights of Stoodley Pike

Mind you, it's true to say that those people in the valley have given the Old Fellow a good crack of the whip ever since, so there were no hard feelings. What's more, he even kept a pied-à-terre in the district, right below Stoodley Pike in fact. Down there, they reckoned, the Devil and his cohorts would have their revels, and maybe all those monuments were put up there just to try and put a cap on it. That old cairn, for instance; most of the time it was fine, but

on occasion something would happen that would dislodge some of its stones and then some funny stuff would start. People might see a fiery light shooting out of the cairn, and on the farms below the old Pike cream mightn't churn, oatmeal might rot, horses might go lame, cows might get the 'turn in the head' and foxes might get the chickens. Nothing would go right for those poor hill folk till one of them went up and put the cairn right.

When they finally dug up the old cairn and found some old black bones in the peat beneath it, the old-timers nodded their heads. 'Well,' they agreed, 'we did say as there were imps up to no good with their Master below there, di'n't we?'

The tower that rose in place of the cairn in 1815 to commemorate the end of the Napoleonic Wars was the result of Quaker fundraising. It should have been solid enough to resist any disturbance – especially as a young boy's blood had been spilt during the Masons' opening ceremony – but it wasn't. On the day that England was about to fall into another foreign war, in 1854, the tower collapsed. 'Ah,' said the old-timers, 'that there peace monument that the Quakers put up, it takes its job seriously, dunnit?'

Nobody's seen fiery lights issuing from the pike recently, not that I've heard, at least. But there are still other strange lights up on that hillside. Thirty years ago I was told that if you're up there on a foggy night you might see a blue light shining from the hillside below the pike. That means the door to the fairy realm is open. There are plenty who'll tell you of strange lights they've seen in the area, and they'll tell you of the time aliens abducted a police officer in Todmorden and the many reports of unidentified lights in the skies round about, and there are others who'll tell you of the geological faults on that hillside and how when the rocks on the fault move, you might see strange lights appear.

One thing's for sure: Stoodley Pike has never been short of a tale to tell and people are rarely lost for words when they see it.

Sixteen

LIQUORICE AND LOSS

I enjoy visits from my friend Lucie. She likes to pass on odd stories or scraps of folklore that she comes across, and that makes for a good excuse to break off from whatever work I'm doing and settle down for a natter. Today, I was glad to leave the Devil behind and hear what she had to tell me.

'Ey, John,' she announced as I was putting the kettle on, 'I've just been over Pomfret way, meeting an old friend, and she's a great one for stories too. I heard a few things there I thought you'd like...'

Pontefract Cakes

'Pontefract, eh – the fractured bridge, that's where its name comes from, in Old French. What caused its bridge to break, I wonder? My auntie used to like Pontefract Cakes. Whenever we went to visit her, that's what we'd take – a big bag. I sometimes wondered if she really liked them so much that no other gift would do, but it wasn't my place to ask.'

'Ah well, there's worse things. Liquorice has been used for medical treatment for centuries, and used in moderation it's really good for all sorts of things. Like digestion, for instance, and other upsets down there – keeps you regular, you know... Not surprising it's a laxative, as I'm told it needs a lot of pure manure, if you take my meaning, to get it growing. And they use it to make the flavour of other medicines easier to bear, too. Your auntie could always have used her Pomfret Cakes to make Spanish, if she didn't eat 'em, I suppose, though they might take a bit o' soaking. Liquorice root's better. You know about Spanish, o' course…'

'Lucie, of course I do. Water shaken up with liquorice to make it a bit tastier.'

'And folk used to drink it especially when they were taken to some natural mineral spring on Spaw Sunday, to take away the natural flavour! Some of these spaw wells that people used, they were a bit sulphurous, and whatever benefit it may have done you and your innards, the water didn't taste too good. Even the ones that weren't sulphurous didn't always taste too good. So they stuck the liquorice into it – twigs, or sticks usually, or I'm sure Pontefract's local delicacy would have sufficed.'

I had to laugh at that. 'Delicacy isn't the word for 'em! Why ever do they call 'em cakes? Little hard discs of solid liquorice the size of an old penny don't really fit people's idea of a cake!'

'If you're going to ask why they call them cakes, you might as well ask why they call them Pontefract!'

'But I know that too, Lucie, it's because they used to grow liquorice there. Though I'm not sure why such an exotic plant got to be grown on an industrial scale in a small West Yorkshire town.'

'Aye, and that's what I'm coming to. Nobody really knows. Some say the Lacys – they're the lords that built the castle – may have brought it back with them from the Crusades, or that the monks at the priory, with their continental connections, brought it in. But others reckon the Earl of Shrewsbury introduced it as a kind of economic diversification programme in the 1560s – I think that seems the most historically founded. But there's another tale I like better, that says Pontefract got it from the Spanish Armada!'

I nodded, while I poured the tea. 'Right, so there's the "Spanish" in it, I suppose!'

'Exactly. But the happy marriage o' Pontefract and liquorice needed a go-between of course, so we have a schoolmaster from the town who's off t' the seaside for 'is holidays, for a breath of healthy fresh air and a bracing stroll upon the sands somewhere. No idea where it was, I'd like to think it were Mablethorpe or Filey in line with the Wakes trips of my schooldays, but anyway it was somewhere with rocks as well as sand, so we could be talking anywhere along that coast. Anyway, it doesn't matter where, the thing is he was at the seaside and he thought he'd go and take a look at a wrecked Spanish galleon that people were talking about, that had foundered on the rocks.'

'That's the proper schoolmasterly thing to do, of course, spirit of enquiry and all that.'

'Indeed, John, and he were a proper schoolmaster for sure, because walking along that beach he came across a bundle of what looked like twigs washed up on the shore, and he picked them up. They were thin and pliable, and his first thought was "They'd be good for thrashing the boys", so he picked them up and that was his souvenir from the seaside for his pupils'. Lucie paused to swig from her mug, wiped her mouth, and continued.

'Well, of course, it wasn't too long before he had occasion to thrash one of his boys, and he was delighted with his new toy. The twigs had dried out a bit and were light and whippy, and to his great satisfaction the boy seemed to find it a great discomfort. "Well," he thought, "they'll think twice before they misbehave now I have this!" And he swung his new birch hard and keen, so that splinters flew off and fell to the ground. And the boys cried – or rather, tried not to cry – and they grabbed these splinters to bite down on, to ease the sting. And you know, that was no bundle of twigs that the teacher found, but a bunch of liquorice root! So they discovered something as they gnawed the bits of the master's birch… the wood was sweet, and that helped no end to make the pain bearable!'

'O, the sweetness of pain, eh?'

'Umm – let's not go there, Johnny boy… and not only did it make the pain easier to bear, but the sweetness of the twiggy roots lasted longer than the smarting on their backsides.'

'Pain outsmarted by pleasure… So I suppose the teacher and the boys came to a sort of unspoken agreement, each gaining satisfaction by a completely different route?'

'Aye, that's right. Actually, when you think about it a bit, it's a dubious sort of story, i'n't it?'

'In more ways than one! Still, they knew how to make their own amusements in those days, as my auntie always used to tell me. And I wonder how might this tale stand up to the scrutiny of history? From what I know, liquorice was being grown in Pontefract in the 1200s, and the Armada was 1588!'

'Was it now? 800 years of liquorice, eh? Enough to give Pomfret Cakes a local designation in the EU, I'd say!'

'So how did they get from the cane to the cake, Lucie?

'Oh yes! Well, that was down to the schoolmaster's enthusiasm, too. Those fragments of twig – of course they were liquorice – that were scattered about the floor were swept out of the schoolroom at the end of the day and the sandy soil of Pontefract really suited them. So they took root and there you go! An industry! Pomfret folk were so jealous of it that growers were forbidden to give away any bits of root. And somewhere in all this the Pontefract Cake was invented. So there!'

I put a couple of slices of an equally local Yorkshire treat in front of us – ginger parkin, a lot more like cake, to my mind, than the Pontefract ones – and refilled Lucie's mug as we sat down with our tea. She leaned across the table.

'Any road, that weren't the tale I wanted to tell you. The one I got's a sad one, though. Would you like to hear that?'

'Any story worth remembering is worth the telling, Lucie.'

THE GIRL IN THE WATER

'Right, well, it's only short, and it comes from an old song that were written about the middle o' th' nineteenth century, so it's supposed t' be true. It's about a young girl called Mary, and she lived at a mill near Pontefract. She worked there as a maid and everyone liked her as she was sweet and I guess a bit of a dreamer, from what we hear in the rest o' this tale.

'One of her jobs was to draw water from the millstream. It frightened her at first, as when she came to the mill, she'd had a dream, a nightmare really, but one that had truly felt real. In the dream she saw a body tumbling along in a stream of water, turning over and over, and she'd come to in a bit of a lather, like. But it were one o' th' basic jobs of a maid so she had to do it, and gradually she got used to it and laughed at how fearful she'd been at first. Because, in truth, she'd got to enjoy it. You know what it's like in summat like a mill race, even if there aren't many of 'em around any more – it's a fast-flowing stream, channelled so that it races down to the waterwheel, and it makes a lovely gurgling, tumbling sort o' noise. Mary found the sound of it really fetching.

'There's this deep undertone that flowing water has, you know, and it can be quite hypnotic. So she used to sit there a while, stare at the waters and allow herself to daydream. And sometimes if she wasn't working, when time and weather allowed, she'd go and sit there, for she loved the mood it put her in, the sense of peace and a world beyond. The babbling of the water would seem just like that, a babbling, with words and all, and sometimes she would lean closer to try and hear the words.

'Well, I'm sure you can guess what's coming. There came a day, a warm evening actually, as Mary sat for a while after work, and that night the words were particularly alluring, as if speaking directly to her heart, and she leaned closer over the bank as she really thought she could almost hear those words. Who knows, maybe she thought it were the fairies and she might be able to eavesdrop on their conversations. Maybe she thought they were talking to her, or maybe she was just a little bit hypnotised, entranced even, by that sound. There she was, rocking to and fro with the singing of the waters, almost a part of their song, when she came to – but too late, 'cos there she'd slipped off the bank and suddenly, as she fell into the water, she remembered her dream. The voices were all around her now, and she cried out as she heard them because she understood, and they told her of her past and of her future, and that future was none too bright nor long. There was a body turning over and over as the water raced and it was hers. The voices sang and Mary tumbled, and the big millwheel greeted her with a shudder; it hesitated, just

for a moment, but it was already too late to stop, so it turned on.
Through on the other side came that girl, the voices quiet now,
the body bloodied and lifeless, shattered by her passage through
the wheel.

'An' of course, those at the mill talked, after this tragedy, of
things they remembered. They recalled how Mary had used to talk
of her fears about the stream, and how they used to laugh at her
and told her not to be silly. And how she'd grown to love sitting
by those waters and she'd tell them of the voices she heard, and
they'd laugh at her again. But they'd not laugh at her now because
they all knew that sound of voices barely heard amongst the chatter of water. And now, they all said in lower voices, when they went
to the stream, the waters sounded a bit different – for they could
hear another voice, like a higher, dreamy voice of a young girl, and

they swore it was Mary calling to them. Aye, and nobody felt like lingering there any more.'

Lucie stopped and we picked up our teacups. The tea had got a bit cold, I have to say.

'Sounds a bit like a Jenny Greenteeth story, that.'

'Aye, if you were in Lancashire, but a water spirit like Jenny prefers still water with weed growing on it; she's got a cousin, mebbe, in Yorkshire called Grindylow, likes the same kind o' places. Or there's Peg Powler if you were up in Teesdale, she likes pulling folk into flowing water. But then there are water spirits all over the world ready and waiting to invite you into their world, and I reckon young Mary met one o' those, or a family of 'em, even.'

'We're almost back at boggarts, aren't we, Lucie?'

'Aye, that's reight, John, that's what we talked about last time, i'n't it? And I said you were a bit hard on those of a witchy persuasion. That reminds me, I found another tale about a woman they reckoned were a witch, and I like it better than those tales where she gets some kind o' cruel comeuppance! Put the kettle on again, and let's get some hotter tea…'

Seventeen

KEEPING TO THE OLD WAYS

JENNET BENTON, RIGHT-OF-WAY ACTIVIST

Jennet Benton was another of these women to whom all kinds of malicious rumours attached themselves, and many who knew her as 'the wise woman of Wakefield' spoke differently behind her back than to her face. Not that their gossip stopped them from coming to her cottage in Newton for advice about the weather and the best times for shearing or harvesting, or about something they'd lost, someone whose love they wanted, or someone whose love they did not want. She had all sorts of visitors and she did her best, we can be sure, to send them on with something to show for their visit. It was all to do with the skills she had: some herbalism, some knowledge from observing nature and its patterns, some skill with people and their problems, some personal skills of insight and just maybe something else. It was the 'something else' that people used to talk bad about.

It didn't help that she rather fitted everyone's preconception of a witch – an unkempt appearance, with a fair temper when roused, living in her cottage with a large black cat of equally uncertain temper. It didn't help either that she was a single mother of a son,

George. Back in the 1600s such things made folk talk and the stories got steadily stranger.

One story they told was an old chestnut, really. Sometimes Jennet was away overnight and then, people swore, that old besom that she kept propped up outside the front door – well, just you try looking for it on such nights. You'd not find it and that was evidence for them that she'd flown off on it to some infernal gathering with other women like her.

And that cat of hers – it didn't much like people, and if it left you alone when you visited Jennet that was some kind of a blessing. Many a client left with a scratch or a bite for their pains, especially if they'd tried to pet it overmuch. This was with the exception of one gentleman, a handsome and youngish man who often came to see her. The cat was fond of him over all other visitors, and all in all that suggested that the young man was none other than the Devil in disguise, come a-courting one of his servants. What the heck, it was a good story to tell and it raised an interesting question over George's parentage that the gossips were happy to discuss.

It was a difficult position Jennet found herself in for sure, as it often has been for village wise women or cunning folk of either gender. But she was successful enough to make a living from it for her small family; and whatever people said about her behind her back, it seems she managed to avoid the worst that might happen in her day to a woman accused of witchcraft.

Across the fields from Benton's cottage, at Bunny Hall, lived Richard Jackson, the man who farmed those same fields. Jackson was keen on making the most of his farm, and in his opinion the presence of a path across his land was detrimental to his plans. Those who used it might cause no end of damage or loss to himself. No matter that the path was frequently used, the people who made their way across it were in his way and he announced that – as law allowed – he would shut it down, claiming that its users were damaging his property.

This may sound familiar to us today, of course, and just as now the locals objected. The path was long-established, from 'time out o' mind', and it was old when grandfathers were still lads, etc. But these protestations were all to no avail. Jackson could, so he did, and the path was no more.

Jennet Benton was one of the most vocal opponents of Jackson's plan, which was a matter not just of convenience but livelihood, as it cut off the way across the fields, making it harder for others to visit her for their needs. And closing the path, for Jennet, didn't close the matter. She and George went right on using it.

Inevitably, this led to a confrontation. Jackson was well aware of the trespass and finally sent his servant, Daniel Craven, out to intercept the pair as they climbed over the new fence. Craven attempted to stop them, and it led to a scuffle in which George threw a stone at the hireling, breaking his teeth. Jackson saw his chance, and went straight to the law. The Bentons were charged with unlawful trespass and assault, and a claim for reparation was made on behalf of the servant, which the Bentons could not deny.

This did not bode well for neighbourly relations, as we might expect, but Jackson tried to strike a conciliatory note when he considered the matter was settled. Silly man, we might think, and we'd be right. Jennet immediately launched into a barrage of words, based loosely around, 'How dare you take me to court for walking on a path that people have used for generations, and how dare you stop up an ancient right of way!'

Jackson persevered, and even made her a gift of a kirtle in his attempt to persuade her he wasn't such a bad sort after all. He should have known that only the reopening of the path could assuage her temper, if it could be assuaged at all. 'Hypocrite!' she spat, 'Here's what I think o' thy tawdry offering!'. And tearing the gifted tunic into shreds, she stepped into her home and tossed it on her fire. Then she came straight out of her door again and pointed a finger at him.

'Soon, "Farmer" Jackson, soon you shall know what it is to incur the wrath of Jennet Benton! Let me tell you – within a year and a day, you shall find at what cost you set the law upon me and my own, and from that time to your life's end you shall rue your decisions on that day.' And the door slammed in his face.

Jackson went home shaken and resigned to having an enemy for life. He was also hoping she was less of a witch than the neighbours

made out. He felt easier as the weeks went by and nothing untoward happened to him. He even felt confident enough to mock her
to his wife and friends. But spells take their time to work out, and
it wasn't until six months later that strange things began to happen.
Maybe he should have put up some rowan sprigs in his attic, or
something of iron, like a horseshoe, over his door, like so many of
his more superstitious neighbours did. But he hadn't done that,
and there was nothing to stop the power of Jennet's words.

  His stock began to sicken. The family saw out of the corners of
their eyes black dogs padding around the house, and cats seemed to
find their yard attractive. But strangest of all and most frightening
were the shrieks that were suddenly heard from nowhere, and the
way that things around the house would move of their own accord.
The servants tired of losing their bedclothes at night, of the constant

disturbances, and one by one they left, passing on the reputation of Bunny Hall Farm so that replacement staff could not be found. Robert Jackson retreated into bewilderment and made the best of it. Just twelve months and a day after he'd had the big row with Jennet, the animals started to thrive again, the shrieks fell silent, and everything seemed to return to normal – for a time, at least.

Then one day, Robert came home and called out a greeting to his wife, as usual. But no answering greeting came, which was strange, and he went to see what she was doing. He looked into the kitchen, and she was there at the table, with her back to him, working busily away at something. 'Ah,' he thought 'she seems to be in a bad mood and not talking to me! Well, perhaps I had better not disturb her', and left the room. They met again at supper, sitting down together, when she spoke to him as she cut into her meat.

'Have you had some more trouble, dear, at market or with that Jennet? For I wonder that you have not spoken to me since you returned home.'

'My dear, I greeted you when I arrived, but since you ignored me, I thought it best to leave you to yourself.'

His wife looked up and stared at him. 'Well, husband, I declare it seems like a house of the dead when you do not even speak to me when I address you!'

Robert's jaw dropped and he made sure his wife was looking when he next spoke, and they realised she had gone deaf! This was bad enough, but a couple of nights later their child was taken with fits. It seemed the bad luck had come back, and this time it was personal. Though his wife soon regained her hearing, Robert himself was the next to suffer fits. He complained sorely of feeling like he was being torn into shreds at the heart, back and shoulders – perhaps just like Jennet had torn up the kirtle – and of hearing things. 'Can you not hear the bells? Why are they ringing? And who is that dancing?'

His wife and son looked at each other, amazed, for they could hear nothing, but so many strange things had happened to them in the last year that they were becoming resigned to such a life. When they heard something outside groan heavily three times, and then the sound of dogs throwing themselves with much barking and snarling against the doors, the family finally began to talk of remedial measures. Surely, they concluded at last, there was some connection with Jennet Benton, and they had surely felt her wrath, as she had promised. Now was the time, they decided, to lay at the woman's door a charge of witchcraft.

Soon after, something like a deputation banged loudly on the Bentons' door and accused Jennet of witchcraft. She laughed. They threatened her with penalties and still she laughed.

'It's true,' she said 'Farmer Jackson and I did fall out and yes, I did curse him. Wouldn't you? How many of you have not cursed someone whose actions have wronged you? But curse as you will, and curse as I might, there is nothing of the sort that I can do. No, gentlemen, look not at me for these travails, but look to God. For it is God who, as the Good Book tells us, looks to the plight of the poor, and the unprotected, and surely it is God who brings this warning to Farmer Jackson and all of you! If the farmer wants an end to his troubles, he must look to himself and to restitution!'

The Jacksons had already persuaded the officers of the law that the Bentons had a case to answer, however, so on 7 June 1656, Jennet and her son George appeared at York Assizes, accused of witchcraft. The jury listened to the travails of Farmer Jackson and to the reputation of Jennet Benton, considered the matter carefully, and sent Jennet and George back home, acquitted.

Maybe they thought something like this: Jennet Benton may have had the makings of a neighbour from Hell, but who did the Devil's work in this case? And in the end, whose side are you on? The greedy or the dispossessed?

Eighteen

THE WRONG KIND
OF PARTY

The fairies know which side they're on, and it's mostly their own, but there are times when perhaps the interests of the little people and ours coincide, and that's when we might indeed call them the Good Neighbours.

Certainly we hear tell of changelings, when the fairies steal a human child and replace it with one of their own – a kind of cultural exchange scheme that's never gone down too well with humans, as fairy children have tended to be fractious and have 'development issues'. We hear tell of fairy malice, like shooting arrow bolts at people that cause some hard-to-diagnose ailment. And we've already heard of the fate that befell Sam when he mocked a local boggart, and boggarts are closer kin to the fairies than we. Yet we also hear tales of kindness given out by the fairies to humans who either respect them or whose lives seem, to fairy eyes, blighted by other humans' unkindness. So it seems, from all the stories you hear from all the centuries of all the people who meet fairies, or elves, or even boggarts, that you need to be on guard a bit when you meet their kind – but don't anticipate either fey friendship or malice, because it all depends on your own actions.

Bad Neighbours and Good Neighbours

Whatever you do, you don't mock them or take their name in vain. That's a lesson that Rob o'Harry'o't'Deans never learned. Rob – let's drop his full name which is, after all, something of a mouthful – lived in Walsden and he was one of those neighbours that we can do without. Not someone like Jennet Benton, with a hard tongue and uncertain temper, but who will nevertheless stand up for her community, but someone who's weasely and dishonest. We all know them, surely – those people who are ready to lift something that's not theirs and then swear blind they're innocent.

That's the kind of neighbour Rob was. Anything left outside for more than a few minutes was likely gone if Rob was anywhere about. You'd mention it and there he'd be, tut-tutting and shaking his head, full of sympathy. He'd even help people to look for their things, since it was quite plain that people were looking suspiciously at him, but if they said anything he acted all injured. No one could catch him in the act and nobody could find the missing goods in his house, so there was no proof, no evidence they had against him, but there was plenty of distrust.

Rob believed in fairies, or at least what he said suggested he believed in them, because as he sympathised with someone over some lost item, he'd say something like, 'Aye, 'tis funny 'ow things disappear like that, ennit, and ne'er sin nor fahnd agen. Ah reckon it mun be the feeries…'

Maybe his neighbours believed in fairies, but that didn't mean they believed Rob. And as for the fairies themselves – well, they heard him talking like that and they weren't too happy to be spoken ill of for none of their doing. However, given their policy of not interacting with humans too obviously and giving the game away, there wasn't a lot they could do about it. So they bided their time, disapproved of Rob and his doings and sayings, sympathised with his neighbours and kept an eye on him.

But nobody is all bad. Rob, for all his pilfering, anti-social ways and weasely words, wasn't that nasty a person in himself. If you met him at the inn you found, for all your doubts, that here was a man who could tell a good story – the sunnier side of his lies, if you like – and could keep a group of drinkers entertained for an evening. He did supplement his income with a bit of honest work, weaving at home like many of his neighbours, and he took care to be honest where it was likely to be double-checked.

Rob did indeed like a drink, and if he could have a drink and good company and pay for it after with a bit of thieving, that was a good night for him. Back in his day, which was maybe a couple of hundred years ago, people used to walk around the hills rather more than we do today, often in connection with work, and the country inns were fuller than they are now.

There was one night Rob came across the hill to Mankinholes, another little hillside village, and he supped till it was quite late. It was dark and quiet when he set off home and that suited him fine. He didn't disturb the villagers as he found his way into one of their storerooms and came out with a couple of pieces of worsted. He didn't go home by the wider lanes, though – he kept to the moor edge, along one of the old packhorse tracks which he knew well, just picked out in the faint moonlight. And that's when the fairies saw their chance.

The track makes its way across the hillside through a scatter of rocks tumbled down from the slope above over the centuries, and among these rocks was one called the Eaves Stone. It stands on the edge of a flattish piece of land and as Rob was coming up towards the stone, he thought he heard something ahead of him. Instinctively, he ducked down and scurried over to the shelter of the stone. He listened awhile – what he heard sounded like someone was having a bit of a bash, laughing and giggling and a bit of a crash of crockery, and some fine music to go with it too. What a time to have a do like that, and what a place! Amazed, Rob was curious. Carefully, he removed his clogs so he wouldn't make any noise, and inched himself up to the top of the stone.

What he saw raised his eyebrows! If he'd only made it seem like he believed in fairies before, here was a sight to make his mind up. It was a fairy feast, a celebration of some sort. There was a long table set up with a lantern on a pole at its centre and all around it

were sat little folk, dressed to the nines, with cups and dishes set in front of them. They all seemed to be having a thoroughly good time. There was a little band playing away, with musicians playing a jaw harp, flute and a small drum, and some of the party-goers were kicking their legs up as they danced to the music. Rob felt something of a hankering to join them, but his amazement – and something like fear – held him back.

So he lay there, peeping over the edge of the rock, and kept as still as possible. To one side of the gathering an old man played with fairy children, blowing great big bubbles from a pan, and the children chased them, laughing, as the bubbles floated up and away towards the moor. The bubbles floated straight towards the stone where Rob was lying, in fact, and they burst against the rock and spattered into Rob's face. He could do without that, as he nearly sneezed and gave himself away, and ducked down again. Well, the fairies looked set up for the night and Rob began to get sleepy. After all, he thought, he'd had a lot to drink that night and the fairies would surely be off before daybreak – he could get on home safely then. He laid his head on his arm and went to sleep.

Well of course, the fairies knew all about him there behind the rock, and as soon as they knew that they had sent him to sleep the old man clapped his hands and several of the younger ones scurried around behind the Eve Stone. They had no fear of waking Rob – he'd be asleep till the morning was properly come. And they put the clogs back on his feet and they laid one piece of worsted under his head for a pillow and the other under his arm. As the first light began to show they all dispersed, well pleased with themselves.

People were up and about early in those days, and once day came the packhorse tracks got busier. It wasn't long before someone came across Rob sound asleep there by the rock and got suspicious about the worsted packs he was snuggling up to. So they went off and called people in, and when Rob awoke, it was with some very stern-looking men around him. Nobody heard the fairies laugh, as he was arrested and taken off to Halifax.

And that's the last anyone in the area saw of Rob – whether he ended up his days in York Prison or Australia, or some even more unpleasant fate, I don't know, but surely he remembered that night at the fairy feast until his last moments.

Nineteen

THE ROCKY ROAD OF LOVE

On the other side of the valley from Rob's nemesis stands a double outcrop of rocks nearly a ¼ mile in length, overlooking the three valleys that join at Todmorden. It's a bleak spot, but some days it is quite a hive of activity, with climbers scrambling up the rock faces and a regular stream of walkers passing by. The climbers have their sights set on various rock faces along the edge, but the walkers usually head for one particular spot – the Bridestone, the very stone that the whole area is named for. And with good reason; the Bridestone is unique in West Yorkshire – a natural standing stone shaped like an upturned bottle, a huge teardrop-shaped mass of millstone grit perched on a narrow pedestal, edge on to the prevailing wind. She isn't the only weirdly shaped rock in the vicinity – the imaginative visitor can see a sphinx, whelk shells, a tortoise and all kinds of other characters worn into the craggy sandstone – but she's the only one about whom there is a traditional narrative.

One version of the story says this is where the first marriage in Todmorden took place, hence the 'bride' name. The boulder lying on the ground beside the Bride is similarly named the Groom. However, this may just be an outsider's sniping comment on what they considered the rough-and-ready ways of Todmorden past.

A Marriage Hits the Rocks

Yet the full story is along similar lines, it must be said. It concerns a pair of young people who met and fell in love. For the sake of the story we'll call them Nan Moor and Jack Stone. I don't know where Jack was from, but Nan lived in a little cott at one end of the Bridestones range; a quirky little house constructed between two massive upstanding slabs of rock, so the couple were already set up with somewhere to live when they decided to spend their lives together. They didn't bother with the church though – they felt that the stones themselves were as symbolic a place to make their vows as any building, and they only needed themselves and a few friends, not a priest. The couple of upstanding stones known as the Bride and Groom were surely an appropriate site for their declarations.

So one day they stood between the two stones and laid a hand each on either stone and swore to be true to each other and that their love would be as steadfast as the stones. That, to all intents and purposes, was their wedding, and I doubt very much if it was the first time that kind of arrangement had been made in the area.

But that doesn't concern us. What concerns us is the happy couple, living up there in splendid isolation in a tiny cottage among the rocks and winds of the Bridestones. They both went hither and thither for bits and pieces of work, and fetched up home when done. But there were some days when either through work or weather there was nothing to be done but stay at home. In the early days that was fine, but as familiarity grew between them, so did a certain amount of claustrophobia. Jack, for his part, began to feel that there was better enjoyment to be had drinking with his mates in one of the inns round about, and it got later and later that he rolled up the hill to his home. By that time neither of them were in the most balanced of moods. In short, their union ran into bickering, into argument, into resentment. The magic was gone, and with it the peace of their tiny home. After one especially fierce argument, Jack stormed out into the night and stamped down into Todmorden.

On the way, his mind was filled with a mixture of anger, despair and questions. How had he got himself into this situation? He'd loved Nan, and she him – so why were they now a torment to each other? Where were the smiles and the quick caresses, when had they stopped? Why couldn't they let each other be free, why was she so upset at him spending time with his friends? Why did she always fly off the handle so easily? What could he do about it? Well, as many a married or near-as couple know, these are questions that are common enough, and most of us will think about them a lot during our lives, but they have no answer.

Down at the inn in Todmorden, his friends had no answers either. 'You married her, Jack, or as good as, and as me old mam said, you make your bed, you have to lie in it.' More sympathetic mates clicked their tongues and shook their heads as Jack recited his complaints about the situation. All other topics of conversation were impossible, and even those who advised resignation to his situation tried to be supportive to their friend. 'Ah, getting hitched to a woman, it's like a ball and chain,' said one, 'they pull us in wi' their pretty ways, but they don't look so pretty once they've got yer'. 'Ah reckon it's a trap devised by Satan hisself,' said another, a single man, 'or God playin' a tricksy game wi' us fellas. Ah can't figure out why any of us fall for it time and again, but we do, aye, we do. Gi' me a single life any day', and he sang a little song:

I'll bide single, single an' free
Ne'er be downcast, happy I'll be
Jack the lad so happy and free
That love will never ever conquer me.

The friends clapped and commended him on his sentiments. 'Ah, you're right there,' they agreed, 'marriage is summat good for no man! Why, it drives us to drink, see!'. And they laughed – all except Jack Stone.

'Aye, you're right an'all. It's not Nan, though she's bad enough, it's getting wed that's the trouble! If we hadn't wed, maybe Nan and I would still be getting on alright. What is it that tricks us into this iniquitous prison for our souls?' Some of the lads blinked at this unexpected turn of rhetoric, but Jack hadn't stopped. 'You know, it's them darned stones that did for us! Standing up there, Bride and Groom they call 'em, giving us ideas that go against the grain of free men and women. Ah, those stones mock us as much as the priests do, and like those fancy-frocked praters they deserve to be cast down upon the ground for misleading us poor folks into denying our true nature – to be free lovers, not partners in bondage! Are ta with me, lads?'

Wide-eyed and unsure where this new-found eloquence was leading, all they could do was stammer, 'Oh, aye, er... aye, right, Jack, yer right…'

'Then I say we throw off their yoke and cast them down tonight! Let us strike a blow for our freedom and the freedom of our brothers and sisters!'

This was good, stirring stuff, and other men in the pub had stopped talking and were turned round and listening. They egged Jack on. This looked like turning into the best evening they'd had for some time. Parroting cries of 'Strike!', 'Freedom!' and 'Aye, cast 'em down!' echoed round the pub.

'Then go, men of Todmorden, go and get thy picks, get thy hammers or owt else that'll bray a blow for freedom! Go and meet back here, for tonight we shall strike! Oh, and someone bring me a spare, eh, as all my tools up at t'cott…'

As the inn emptied, the landlord wasn't so happy at this turn of events, but there was nothing he could do about it. Half an hour or so later, his inn was full again with men waving a medley of heavy tools, cheering and clustering around Jack.

'Let's go! To the Bridestones!'

'To the Bridestones!'

The crowd streamed out of the inn again and up the hill towards the target of Jack's impassioned oratory. Well primed with drink, this was a rabble and they were roused. They made good time up that hill and before too long were stood, panting, before the Bride and Groom. The two stones loomed large above the men and the moonlight seemed to increase their presence. Breaths were taken, mettles were fettled, and at a word from Jack they all stepped forward and started picking and hammering away at the Groom. Like the Bride, the Groom was joined to its base by only a narrow neck, and it was there that the blows were directed. The sound of iron on stone rang across the hillside and rolled down into town. Folk wondered what was going on.

The Groom knew all too well. It groaned, cracked, swayed and began to topple. Several men had to jump out of the way as its pedestal finally snapped, and the huge bulk crashed to the ground. A ragged cheer went up from the men, 'A first blow for freedom!'

And then it was the turn of the Bride. The men gathered round her. The Bride was taller than the Groom, a slender shape looming high above them, and the moonlight surely enhanced her impressive stature. Whether that was what they were thinking I don't know, but something made them all hold back. The night fell still and silent as they all looked at the now-single sentinel of Jack's vow. Jack felt the momentum slipping away and tried to regain control over the proceedings, 'We're nearly there, men!

Strike hard for our liberty!', and he swung his borrowed pick-axe at the Bride's waist.

The other men drew breath and raised their weapons, but as Jack's pick struck home, just as the ugly crack of iron on stone rang out, an unearthly scream rent the air around them, a piercing wail that seemed to come from the stone itself. The men's hair stood on end, dread filled their hearts, and off they all ran, back down the hill, tumbling into Todmorden and the inn where the landlord was ready to welcome them and offer them whatever comfort they could pay for. Those men talked about what had happened up at the Bridestones that night, and no doubt they told others as well, and that's how this story got to us today.

The remains of the home where this young couple lived can still be seen today. The two rock slabs, engraved with niches to hold beams and a roof, shelf space for its occupants and an outlook across sheep-cropped fields down to where the three valleys meet. And the Bride is still there today, standing beside her prostrate companion. I suppose Jack succeeded in his aim, in a way, as without the Groom standing beside her, no vows can be made standing between them, and of course it takes two to make a marriage.

So was it really the Bride who screamed that night? Or was it Nan herself, standing in the shadows of the rocks, lamenting at the blow that struck her heart?

Twenty

ALL'S WELL THAT ENDS WELL

Someone once asked me, as I was telling some of these tales from our county, 'Aren't there any happy endings in Yorkshire?' Well, there are, for sure, though at times we seem to have more than our fair share of tragedy and unhappiness. We share this with that other great stream of narrative in Britain, the traditional ballads and songs. There's nothing like a Border Reiver's tale, for instance, to make you count your blessings on a rainy day with your roof leaking.

So despite our local fondness for lugubrious phrases like, 'It'll all end in tears' and 'I knew it couldn't last' and despite Ted Hughes once observing that 'Everything in West Yorkshire is slightly unpleasant. Nothing ever quite escapes into happiness', we cannot in all honesty take to our bosoms the notion that West Yorkshire folk are uniquely glum. However, we do seem to get gloomier as the hills get higher in the west – but I blame the weather for that.

Really it's not all that bad, by any means. After all, Jennet Benton was acquitted, the right chap got the prize for killing the boar, Philippa Calverley kept her home, the ghost at the Sun has gone quiet and the fairies may still be at Cottingley. I hope you might take other plusses from the tales in this book too, but if you still need cheering up, you can find plenty of Yorkshire joke books and a wealth of droll dialect poems and stories. Nonetheless, I think it behoves me to finish this collection on an upbeat note, by telling you the tale of Sir William Wentworth Blackett.

The Wanderer Returns

Sir William had been born with an inquiring mind and an imagination set far beyond his compass. These are things we seem to set great store by, in the wider scheme of things, but they can be an unhappy combination for anyone who feels caught within the compass that they exceed – like our hero. Think of an explorer; then think of being married to one. I'm sure it suits some, but whether it suited the wife of Sir William Wentworth Blackett I have my doubts.

'How long is it since they ascertained the world was round, my dear?' he asked one day at breakfast.

'About 300 years, I think, husband' his wife replied, wondering if it was something about the shape of his egg that had inspired such a question.

'A good time, then, some ten generations for us to imbibe the notion thoroughly and digest it completely, wouldn't you say?'

His wife looked at him. She wasn't sure where this conversation was leading, but for some reason she felt uneasy. Was it her imagination, or was the clock ticking more loudly?

'And yet, we still say that we search to the ends of the Earth, eh! Sailors still return to tell us they've been to the end of the world and back, or to the four corners of the world, which is the same thing really, only a lot longer journey, and nobody contradicts them, do they? They don't say, "Sirrah! You cannot have sailed to the ends of the Earth, because the Earth is a ball, and as we know balls have no end! Or corners!" Do they?'

A mystified hush had fallen upon the dining room at old Bretton Hall. The servants beside the table looked at each other; they'd watched William grow up and they could sense one of his projects forming in his mind.

'So we have two tales: one, what the educated folk believe and tell other educated persons – like ourselves – that the world is round, a sphere that always returns upon itself. Two, that the world has ends and corners, and it's not the educated classes that tell us that, but those who have actually been out there! So who's telling the truth, eh? Anybody know? What do you all think?' He addressed his enquiry to the room, but the room merely nodded cautiously.

'Aye, it's a mystery, and mysteries need resolving in this Age of Reason', he muttered and lapsed into silence. In due course the family and servants retired to their other tasks without any more being said, other than the due courtesies of dining, though the atmosphere was surely absent of rancour.

No more was said on the matter for some time, but her lady-ship noted that her husband became distracted and industrious, sending letters and messages to people here and there, taking notes from books, pacing up and down in his library and frequently grunting or expostulating in a way that was unusually hard for her to comprehend, despite her having grown quite accustomed to her husband's many forms of utterance. 'Whatever it is,' she thought, 'I'm sure he'll tell me in good time.' Which Sir William Wentworth Blackett did.

'My dear,' he said one evening when they were alone at the dining table, 'you know that when I have a notion in my head, whether something is fact or fancy, it is sometimes hard for me to settle until I have established to my satisfaction the true state of the matter'. His wife did indeed know that side of his character, and it was something that had attracted her to the union in the first place, despite some disadvantages when she wanted him to think of something more in her areas of concern. She told him so.

'Ah' he said, and paused. 'Well, my dear, I am sure you won't take it as any slight or anything that means that I am other than perfectly delighted with our marriage, and with you personally and with your way of running the household. I am blessed with such a wife!'

'Thank you…' she began.

'But you see, you do remember our conversation about the ends of the Earth?' She inclined her head affirmatively, if questioningly. 'I shall find them! That is my resolve! And if not, then I shall know who has the facts of the matter! I cannot accept hearsay as scientific truth, so I must make the experiment myself! I have located a ship and a good captain and crew, and we sail from Liverpool a week on Monday! This is an exciting scientific project, my dear, and I am sure you are just thrilled to hear of this grand plan!'

She was, of course, far from thrilled and made her feelings quite plain when they were alone later that evening. But it was to no avail, as she well knew. The plans were settled and the grand project was afoot, and though she would be well settled for money in his absence, who knew how long that absence might be?

So on the appointed day off went Sir William Wentworth Blackett, and the household made the best of it. At least things were more relaxed after he'd gone; there was no more pacing, no more chaos of packing, fewer errands for the servants to run. The household settled down, after a fashion, to its new state.

And so the days went by, and so the months, and so the years. The household wondered where he had gone and what had become of their master. Was he still striving to reach the ends of the Earth? Had he overshot them and found himself in some limbo? Was he making a new life somewhere? Or was he dead? Mrs Wentworth Blackett grew lonely and though she had many friends in local society, more comforting company was lacking and safe and discreet alternatives hard to find. Indeed, there were a number of men very keen on persuading her that her husband was surely dead, and that therefore she – and all the property thereby accruing to her – was once more eligible for marriage. She sighed often, and lamented to her maid, 'If only he would return – whether his voyage be rough or smooth at sea, surely it would be nicer here with me! Whether his voyage be windy or fair, it must surely be easier than the blasts that assail me here!'

As did Sir William Wentworth Blackett sigh, as he pursued his dream through land after land, across sea after sea, and he seemed no nearer to his goal. One day he was sitting at a busy Eastern port, gazing at the boat that would take him further yet, and he suddenly felt weary.

'Ah me,' he said to himself, 'so many years, so many miles, so many sights I have seen since I last saw my wife and home, and I declare that right now no sight would be sweeter to me than Bretton Hall. Surely, if there were an end to this Earth, I should have found it by now, and been required to turn back at its limit; but now I am inclined to believe that Columbus was right'. He brooded long into the warm evening, listening to the birds so different from the calls of his childhood, and the language of the people around him, which were so resistant, for a world traveller like himself, to comfortable colloquy.

In the morning he called his crew together and announced that his quest was at an end; they would be returning to England forthwith and may the winds send them swiftly and safely home. The men cheered, for they too were wearying of their employer's obsession and their good cheer spurred on their boat.

Twenty-one years is a long time to be left and Mrs Wentworth Blackett was weakening under the pressure of entreaties from eligible men. She was inclined to agree that so many years, with no word of news, tended to indicate that her husband had met his own end rather than the end of the Earth. She was getting no younger and was looking for both comfort and support in her later years. Finally she acquiesced to one man who had been a good friend and pleasant company to her during her husband's absence. Plans were made for the wedding and the day came, the service was spoken and the new couple and their guests returned to Bretton Hall for the celebrations.

That was the day a ragged man, clothed in a strange array of garments and colours, turned up in the village of Bretton to find the villagers in high spirits. It was all talk of the marriage up at the hall, and no one showed him the respect due to a master. His travels had taught him how to live on little, to set little store by appearance as long as clothes did their job, and the sun and the wind had lined and tanned his face. He had lost the English gentleman's self-consciousness, and it showed. Sir William Wentworth Blackett

looked down at himself and saw himself with unaccustomed eyes. 'Hmm… little different from a beggar, to be sure.' And an idea began to form. 'Ha! I dare say my wife would be appalled, but none more so than her imagined groom, I wager, and I'll soon put the smile back on her face!' Away he strode to his old home on the edge of the village.

Soon he was knocking at the back door and craving indulgence on behalf of the happy couple and himself. The servants were terse, but they brought the beggar into the kitchen and put some bread and scraps from the table before him with a tankard of beer. Sir William ate and drank, thanked the servants, and stood up. 'Tradition demands that I drink to the new bride's health and happiness!', and off he went, through the corridors he knew so well, to the drawing room where the guests were assembled. The servants, horrified, pursued him and wrestled with him at the door. But if his travails hadn't improved Sir William's appearance, they had certainly honed his strength, and quite a skirmish erupted. Naturally, despite the noise of the wedding party, it soon became apparent that there was a disturbance; the lady and her new husband threw open the doors. 'What in God's name is going on here?'

Sir William Wentworth Blackett shrugged off the servants and stepped into the room. The guests stared. 'A boon, my lady, I ask of thee – a glass of wine to drink thy health and future happiness.'

'You'll have none of the sort!' said the lady, recognising the beggar no more than anyone else had; but as her new husband stepped forward, her old husband quickly slipped into a chair at a dining table and sat down. The guests raised their eyebrows even further, but began to appreciate the party a lot more.

'My lady, I think you will surely grant me my request – just a small glass, more regretted in its denial than its acceptance, you may find.'

Was this a veiled threat? A silence followed and then a nod, and a bottle was brought to where Sir William sat, holding a glass he'd picked up from the table. Sir William bowed his thanks and grabbed the bottle from the servant's hands. The guests gasped –

this was getting ever more interesting! Sir William drank a glass, toasting the lady's health, and then he refilled the glass and raised a new toast to her future happiness, drank it down and threw his arms around the lady, kissing her.

Uproar! Finally, he was subdued, none too smoothly or peacefully, and Sir William Wentworth Blackett decided it was time to speak up.

'Kind people!' he cried, 'Do not judge too harshly, for I am merely claiming my own! For is this not my own true wife, deserted, through my ill judgement, for over twenty years? Pray, sirs, take a look if you will at the ring I wear about my neck. I am William Wentworth Blackett and I have returned home!'

His wife peered more closely at his face and behind the lines and the greying hair she saw the features of the man she had married so many years before. Her eyes widened, her skin went pale and she sat down. She glanced at the man she had only that day married – he was as pale as she and his shoulders were visibly drooping. The hands holding him down relaxed their grip and Sir William stood up.

'I am, as you see, safe and sound though rather worse for apparel, most sorry for my long absence and most distressed to disrupt this wedding party…' he glanced at the man whose hopes had just been dashed. 'But let's have no more reproof! No more blame! Let us have reunion, forgiveness, and as we have a celebration prepared, let us celebrate! Friends, I raise a glass again – let us drink to the delight of a good wife, a good home and the joy of homecoming!'

The unlucky groom did not stay long, nor the guests who felt close friendship with him; but the friends of the Wentworth Blacketts and the servants in their rooms stayed long and talked much. The very next morning, Mrs Wentworth Blackett took the boots and hat Sir William had been wearing and put them aside, and for many years after, even after the couple had gone to their own long sleep, they were still shown to guests as a memento of the wedding that never was.

Afterword

BACKGROUNDS AND REFLECTIONS

There are all sorts of narratives that we come across in folklore, ranging from the rather grand world of myths, down through the semi-removed reality of legends, the everyday world of personal memory and so on to the anecdotes and jokes that enliven our conversation. In traditional stories the different types can appear and mingle together, or sustain a short narrative on their own. Much depends on the context, and this is a crucial element in any story. When we tell a joke with friends, we don't tell just any joke, but one that fits the conversation we are having. This also goes for a personal anecdote, unless it is used to start a conversation in which case it is often framed in a special way to draw our listeners' attention and get their honest feedback, rather than their mockery (as tales of ghosts, fairies and UFOs are often treated). We might tell a story to illustrate an opinion in a discussion, thus avoiding a direct confrontation with another's view. Stories may change depending on who we're with, and when and where we're telling them. If you're a performing storyteller there's more incentive to tweak a tale to improve your performance or audience response, a temptation that must always be approached with utmost care that no vital motif or ingredient of truth is damaged in the process.

This is the constant dynamic behind the human passion for telling stories of one kind or another. When we hear these stories, it
is the context in which we hear them that we should take note of.
Some of the stories in this collection have come from books or
personal letters, but around half have been told to me by people I
have met, perhaps in a pub or café, on a walk, or at one of the talks
I regularly give to various local societies. Such a source is always a
boon, as it indicates that a traditional tale is still alive and ready to
be told again and again, as long as there is an audience for it. If you
are reading this, it's evidence that there *is* an audience.

The tale in my first chapter is indeed true, related – without
embroidery, I can assure you – as a personal memory of a strange
experience. Thankfully I wrote down everything about that experience at the time, so I can be sure I have not twisted the events over
the intervening thirty years, as would be so easy to do as the memory's immediacy fades. Moreover, some of it's in the papers: articles
relating to the deer can be found in the *Hebden Bridge Times* for
5 December and the *Evening Courier* of 8 December 1980. As
those thirty years have passed, I can now see the events less personally, allowing the experience to become a narrative in its own
right; and this may offer a glimpse into the genesis of other stories.
Looking back, I can urge that whenever anything odd happens to
you, write it down as soon as you can, before you start to tell other
people about it!

Other than personal experience, stories and folklore can be
recovered from a variety of sources. One such resource is diaries.
Oliver Heywood (1630-1702) was a controversial Nonconformist
minister who kept a full journal of his daily life and doings,
thoughts and opinions. Inevitably, Heywood came into contact
with, and sometimes wrote about, beliefs about the witchcraft and
folk magic around him (Chapter 3). It does not matter whether we
believe in magic or think the witches of old were falsely accused;
for uncountable numbers of people throughout the world today,
magic and the 'supernatural' in general, is an accepted, if often
unwelcome, part of life and I don't think we should dismiss such
concepts too readily. Even when people make prayers to effect

some change in their lives through the workings of a spiritual being, they are still, in essence, accepting the principles of magic. Like many before and after them they are attempting to put those principles into practice.

There have always been people popularly supposed to hold some special knowledge by which change can be caused through non-rational means. Often these people worked for their local communities. We may call them priest, minister, or imam, but if they worked outside the religious frameworks, then they were usually known in Britain as witches or cunning folk (Chapters 2, 11, 13, 17). The latter, through some occult knowledge or reputation, offered their services to remove suspected malefic witchcraft from a sufferer and were thought to be generally helpful. Typically they also told fortunes, found lost items or people, conjured or dispelled love, brought retribution on thieves, made protective charms and assisted with a wide range of medical needs from wart-curing to cancer. Up until the end of the nineteenth century at least, everyone would have known of a cunning man or woman in their vicinity, whether they liked it or not. Some had wide reputations or were known for some special efficacy; others were astrologers, herbalists or possessed some recognised skill. At times when doctors were too expensive and religion was too plain to raise much hope of spiritual intervention, cunning folk were popular healers for a wide range of human concerns. They were not necessarily so different from witches, who often also offered such services – except in the matter of public opinion. When perceptions turned negative, the charge of witchcraft was never far from any magically inclined woman or man.

Mother Helston (Chapter 2) and Jennet Benton (Chapter 17) were, in the context of these traditional tales at least, women who fell between these two camps of public opinion. As for Betty (Chapter 3), who may or may not have turned into a black cat, we only hear the slanderers' side of the story.

Jennet Benton provides an interesting example of how assumptions can change from one period to another. A brief account of this case is included in 'Depositions from the County of York:

Relating to Offences in the 17th century', No.40 in the Surtees Society series (1861), pp.74-75. Frederick Ross makes a meal of the tale in his *Legendary Yorkshire* (Hull, 1892), and it appears in various collections. If we turn to the internet, particularly to sites in the 'new-age witchcraft' fold, we suddenly find statements that Jennet Benton was executed. Presumably these writers are assuming that anyone accused of witchcraft was firstly found guilty, and secondly executed. Although too many innocent people, especially women, suffered at the hands of witchcraft legislation, both assumptions are far from the case. It sometimes seems that some modern-day witches are too ready to assume a mantle of hereditary victimhood. When investigating the history of any ideology, beware – historians will recount its history more accurately than its followers.

'Names have been changed to protect the innocent', as the saying goes, and so it might be in traditional narratives. Neither William Towneley nor Sybil Bearnshaw of the Eagle Crag tale (Chapter 2) have revealed themselves to historical research. As for Nan Moor and Jack Stone (Chapter 19), don't even bother trying to find their records – though you will have more luck chasing up Walter Calverley (Chapter 11), Richard Beaumont (Chapter 14) and some of our other characters. That's not to say things happened to them exactly as they are related here (Chapter 14), although the story of the Elland Feud (Chapter 13) is as broadly historical as possible from the sources.

This celebrated episode appears in various books and ballads over the centuries, and incidental details vary from narrative to narrative. Yet its veracity is confirmed in documents of the time and Sir John de Eland's murder at Brighouse was probably in October 1350, his son's death following the next year. The sources I have used here include 'The Eland Tragedy: Revenge upon Revenge', a ballad transcribed around 1650, but thought to date from earlier (and from which the quoted quatrain is drawn); J.M. Kaye, 'The Eland Murders, 1350-51' (Yorkshire Archaeological Journal 51, 1979); James Burnley, *Yorkshire Stories Re-told*; Philip Ahier, *The Legends & Traditions of Huddersfield & District, Vol. 2*

(1943), which includes a Tudor account of the events; and Revd John Watson, *The History of the Town and Parish of Halifax* (1789).

There are other definite historical events among our stories too. 'Old Calverley' (Chapter 11) virtually set off a publishing phenomenon, his misdeeds appearing in numerous publications with certain variations in detail about his life, the reasons for and sequence of his mental breakdown, and supernatural occurrences attributed to his restless spirit. It was even the subject of a play, *The Yorkshire Tragedy*, which some people have claimed was the work of Shakespeare! It was probably written by Thomas Middleton, but because of the Shakespeare rumour it frequently appears in collections of apocrypha associated with the Bard. Distinguishing the actual facts of an episode this far removed is impossible, and we may assume elements of truth in each of the varying perspectives – this is the assumption I have made in my own version.

The story of Mary, the dreamy mill girl near Pontefract (Chapter 16), was taken from Holroyd's 1892 *Collection of Yorkshire Ballads*, in which the editor states that the incident actually happened around 1847. I have tried to suggest a context for the events which is less accidental than implied in the ballad.

Barbara Brandolani, a.k.a. Managassa or Margassa (Chapter 4), reminds us that witches are not a thing of the past. She ran a coven in Manchester and was looking for a spacious temple as a home for their rituals. The deconsecrated Baptist chapel at the crossroads in Heptonstall Slack seemed perfect for what she had in mind, and she attempted to buy it in the summer of 1984. The locals, especially the families of the old congregation, were horrified and vowed to stop her. Brandolani declared she would use her skills to back her prospective purchase. They didn't work, and thanks in part to a donation from Cliff Richard, the old chapel was sold to a retired Baptist minister before the season was out. That didn't stop the rumours and allegations though, and you can follow the saga, a candidate for another modern local legend, in the newspapers or in Paul Weatherhead's *Weird Calderdale* (2005).

It might surprise some readers to find that one of our two tales about fairies is not a fantastic legend, but an actual historical event, albeit based on an experience many will find hard to credit. Chapter 5 deals with the experience of two young girls nearly a century ago, and is certainly a story worth telling. For a while, the pictures they took on the edge of a West Yorkshire industrial village were acclaimed as the first photographic evidence of other-worldly beings amongst us. Media around the world were thrilled, spiritualists were agog, and the girls were stunned into relative silence by all the attention. The whole episode tells of the collision of old-world belief in fairies and the new world of film, the idea that 'the camera that cannot lie' and of the uncomfortable interface between the rationalist and spiritual outlooks on life. In time, it told us that with a little ingenuity the camera can certainly 'lead us down – rather than up – the garden path'.

It also suggests that we tailor what we perceive to fit our more comfortable preferences and how, whenever we think a conclusion is cut and dried, there may still be some point that remains unresolved. Though some people considered the 'confessions' made by the girls and published in *The Unexplained* (December 1982) and *The Times* (9 April 1983) as proof that the photos were a youthful hoax, a question has remained over the last photograph, which Frances always claimed was genuine. A full and sympathetic account of the whole episode, from the original photographs and the Theosophical Society to the eventual 1980s denouement, can be found in *The Case of the Cottingley Fairies* (1990) by Joe Cooper, who was also responsible for the 1982 *Unexplained* article. The photographs themselves are in the National Media Museum at Bradford. Much of the field where the girls claimed some of their encounters took place has recently been lost to housing development.

The Cottingley Fairies were seen as benevolent, and those up near Walsden did no harm in the tale we have, either (Chapter 18). Indeed, when they saw how their own interests overlapped with those of their human neighbours', they did those local people some good by putting a rascal in the way of retribution. For occasional acts of this sort, as well as to keep on their good side, many folk preferred to call the fairies the Good Neighbours.

Boggarts (Chapter 4) are fairy kin, but attract less romance. More usually we hear of them through place names and rumours of their association with certain locations. In that guise, they are one of the most common elements of West Yorkshire folklore, popping up wherever people have felt uncomfortable about some place or event. A few could be friendly by doing odd jobs around the house. You generally had to put up with the odd practical joke, but you could always get rid of them by leaving out a set of new clothes. Generally speaking, boggarts were a nuisance and were likely to be invoked whenever something untoward happened for no obvious reason or visible cause.

There were things you could do to deter disturbances at home, though. Before we had insurance companies, preventive measures naturally took precedence over remedial options. Misfortunes had many potential causes and some – including boggarts – were not necessarily of this world. You could keep the rain out most of the time by attending to the roof and doors, but how to guard against the storm, against God's will? Or against the malevolence of those inclined to harm others, or from unwelcome intrusions from the otherworld realms, or from simple bad luck? Our forebears had a rich array of protective devices and symbols for their houses and persons; such as the horseshoe we still see today, carefully placed stones and special architectural features on buildings. We have come across a few in this book that were known in West Yorkshire, and there are numerous other examples

One persistent symbol through the centuries was the human head (Chapter 6). Certain dwellings around the country have pro-prietorial skulls that are linked to the luck of the house, but here in West Yorkshire carved stone heads with minimalist features are a particularly strong tradition. They were once generally referred to as 'Celtic heads', but locally at least most date from the sev-enteenth and nineteenth centuries. Indeed, they seem to be part of an enduring popular belief, recurring from prehistory to the present, that the human head can intercede with the otherworld on our behalf. As such, they are better seen as part of folklore than archaeology; and rather than call them 'Celtic heads' their appearance would be better described as 'archaic heads'. Sidney Jackson of Bradford privately published one small gazetteer of his work, entitled *Celtic and Other Stone Heads*, in 1973; the only book-length and up-to-date discussion of the topic is my own *A Stony Gaze* (1998).

The image of the severed head has haunted Pennine West Yorkshire for centuries. The two legends associating Halifax with the motif were first recorded by Camden at the end of the sixteenth century. The town's name has been problematic in the past for place name experts, though most seem to agree today on 'area of coarse grass on a slope'. All dismiss the taint of magic and sanctity conferred by the old legends. Yet still the fact remains that the history, lore and architecture of the Halifax area have vouchsafed an extraordinary obsession with the motif of the severed head, though one of the tales I feature here – the holy hair version tale – has a variant that involves hanging rather than decapitation.

Folklore has some famous characters and some of the most renowned appear here. Robin Hood is one of our most celebrated Yorkshiremen, and many tales and legends have grown from his activities, a number of them in modern West Yorkshire. Although later tales have shifted Robin south towards Nottingham, earlier accounts place him solidly in the forest of Barnsdale, which covered a swathe of the old West Riding. The tale retold here is a crucial one, telling of Robin's headstrong and mysterious road to his death (Chapter 8).

Another famous character of traditional lore is the Devil (Chapter 15). We can't claim any kind of Yorkshire precedence for the Old Lad, and I'm sure few in our county would ever have wished to, but like a bad penny he turns up in various tales, in different guises. For instance, in the Calder Valley at Great Rock he's a bit of a lad and underneath old Stoodley Pike he was a dark presence – but even when he isn't named, some might suspect his hand.

They say the Devil gets into men at times, and we certainly have some wicked behaviour in these pages. Yet the worst may be thwarted by calm or quick thinking, as we hear in a gruesome fashion at Illingworth and Sheepridge (Chapter 12). In both these accounts, evil intent remains assumed, but in the latter there is a variant where suspicions are confirmed. Either way, you may never feel the same way about the Sunday roast again. Both Sheepridge variants appear in Philip Ahier's *Legends and Traditions of Huddersfield and District* (1940-43); the Illingworth incident can be found with more background in my own *The Mixenden Treasure* (2009).

Stoodley Pike (Chapter 15) is a prominent obelisk above Hebden Bridge that, despite its devilish associations and prehistoric legacy, owes its current notability to a Quaker peace fund and Masonic symbolism. However, that is only a fragment of its history. A more detailed discussion of the monument, its site, its history and other folklore associated with it can be found in my own *Folk Tales from Calderdale Vol. 1* (2007), which contains other legends from this prolific part of West Yorkshire, each with full background and context.

Another landmark is the Bridestones, the site of one of our grittier romances (Chapter 19). The Bride is a memorable stone – 15ft tall, with about 11ft of that rising up above its waist, teardrop in shape, but angled into the biting Pennine winds like a sail. The Bridestones have been known as such since at least 1491. The 'bride' element is controversial; it may simply mean 'a bride', for some reason now unknown, or it could be a reference to a pre-Christian British goddess known locally as Brigantia – the tutelary deity of the Brigantes tribe who occupied Northern England when the Romans arrived. Brigantia was a goddess, appropriately, of high places, and if she is the origin of the place name (names such as Brigit and Bride have been claimed as variants of the same goddess), then the Bridestones may be best understood as a natural site held sacred in prehistory. With their fantastic formations, the Bride at their head, it certainly exudes an air of otherness. However, it must be admitted that there is inevitably no concrete evidence of such sanctity.

The Bride herself is also known locally and by climbers as the Bottle Neck, as another interpretation of its shape is an upturned bottle. The monument has been much misused by climbers

picking out footholds to try and reach the top of this very chal-
lenging rock. This is not to be encouraged for two reasons. Firstly,
a friend who managed to scale it tells me that it rocks slightly,
meaning that it is cracked and might topple under the strain
of climbing; secondly, if it does fall the valley will lose one of
its unique sights and heritage locations. A notice erected in the
1990s by Calderdale Countryside Services, asking people not to
climb it because of its structural infirmity and local importance,
was vandalised and never replaced.

The rocks which formed the side walls of the cottage in our story
are known to climbers as Big Sister and Little Brother, but their
'official' name is Fast Ends, i.e. earth-fast rocks making the ends
of the house. As the marks indicate, they really were house walls at
one time, standing 19ft apart with the space between enclosed for
a two-storey home. Between 1802 and 1820 it was the home of a
branch of the Stansfield family; a boy who grew up there, Abraham
Stansfield, became a nationally recognised botanist and naturalist,
and attributed his familiarity with flora and fauna to his early experiences being surrounded by nature at such close hand.

Departures, homecomings and obsessive quests lie at the heart
of so many traditional narratives, so this collection of stories ended
with a happy homecoming. Bretton Hall, which stands in what is
now the Yorkshire Sculpture Park, once held on display a hat and
pair of leather boots that became associated with the wanderer in
this tale (Chapter 20). However, they belonged to another wanderer, a Matthew Wentworth, rather than the hero of our version,
and were preserved through the thankfulness of his mother following his long absence. The version here, again sourced from
Holroyd's *Yorkshire Ballads*, comes from a ballad popular in the late
nineteenth century and sung by Jimmy Mann, a pedlar of Scissett.
Even then people were suspicious as to its verity, and Mann was
asked how he'd come by this tale. 'Ah,' he said, 'I made it up, in
1838'. But Jimmy Mann hadn't entirely made up the story, for the
long separation, the random fruitless voyage, the persistent suitors, the beggar's rags and the triumphant homecoming will ring a
bell with those familiar with the Greek classic *The Odyssey*, though

the balladeer was more interested in the homecoming than in the intervening adventures.

Well, there have been plenty of familiar folkloric themes – love stories, tragedies, feuds, murders, ghosts, fairykind, come-uppances, customs and so on – running through this book. And if there aren't any beasts like dragons (though West Yorkshire does have a few rumours of them), there are plenty of familiar animals. Cats, a dog and a deer that a couple of women liked to turn into; a faithful dog that met a tragic end (Chapter 10); and a bona fide wild animal, a wild boar, that is still remembered in the crest of one of our county's historic cities (Chapter 7) all make an appearance. And of course, there are humans of all kinds, to remind us that it takes all sorts to make stories go round, and sometimes, as in this book, they may end on an upbeat note.

Finally, the title of Chapter 14 is in tribute to a favourite record of mine, by Mike Heron. I think it's broadly applicable to that part of social history where it's not so much what you do that matters, but what people think or say you've done. That's what lingers in folklore, and that's what we have in these folk tales from West Yorkshire.

Other titles published by The History Press

Cornish Folk Tales

MIKE O'CONNOR

This collection will appeal to anyone captivated by this beautiful land and its resident kindly giants, mischievous piskeys, seductive mermaids, bold knights and barnacle-encrusted sea captains.

978 0 7524 5066 7

Paranormal West Yorkshire

ANDY OWENS

Poltergeists. UFOs. Murder mysteries. Big cats. Cases of human combustion. Victorian cause célébres. This richly illustrated collection covers a fascinating range of strange events from West Yorkshire's history.

978 0 7524 4810 7

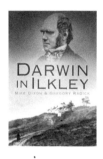

Darwin In Ilkley

MIKE DIXON & GREGORY RADICK

When the *Origin of Species* was published in 1859, Charles Darwin was taking the 'water cure' in the remote Yorkshire village of Ilkley. This title tells the story of his attempts to shore up support for his extraodinary theory during this time.

978 0 7524 5283 8

Mrs Hibbert's Pick-Me-Up and Other Recipes from a Yorkshire Dale

JOANNA MOODY

This collection contains previously unrecorded recipes passed down orally over the centuries, along with snippets of local history and beautiful pen and ink drawings and archive photos.

978 0 7524 5728 4

Visit our website and discover thousands of other History Press books.

www.thehistorypress.co.uk